Stars and Angels

Born in 1916, Michael Stancliffe enjoyed a Lincolnshire childhood with a father who was a parish priest and keen botanist. He read history and took a theology diploma at the Oxford college where Austin Farrer was chaplain, while acting as an undergraduate music critic with Barbara Tatlow, his future wife. Ordained in 1940, he enlivened the parishioners of Watermoor with his productions of religious drama. Subsequently he became chaplain of Westminster School and preacher to Lincoln's Inn.

In 1957 he moved to London as a canon of Westminster Abbey and rector of St Margaret's Westminster, where his sermons drew an appreciative congregation. From 1961 he was also Speaker's Chaplain at the House of Commons.

In 1969 he became Dean of Winchester, where he fostered poetry, music and the visual arts as pathways to God. His awareness of the spiritual power of the Benedictine tradition together with a sense of history and vision for the future led him to establish links between the cathedral and the monastic community of Saint-Benoît-sur-Loire. At the same time, his keen interest in the natural world brought both delight, and the understanding that we must treat the whole creation with consideration. All this together with his gift for words and images found a new outlet in his contributing a regular religious column to the *Daily Telegraph*. His retirement in 1986 was marked by the publication of the (characteristically) neatly titled *Symbols and Dances*. He died the following year, *Jacob's Ladder* being published posthumously.

STARS and Angels

MEDITATIONS FOR THE CHRISTIAN YEAR

MICHAEL STANCLIFFE

FOREWORD BY
SUSAN HOWATCH

MOREHOUSE PUBLISHING

Originally published in English under the title *Stars and Angels* by the
Canterbury Press Norwich, St. Mary's Works, St. Mary's Plain, Norwich,
Norfolk, NR3 3BH U.K.

First American edition in 1997 published by Morehouse Publishing

Morehouse Publishing
P.O. Box 1321
Harrisburg, PA 17105

Morehouse Publishing is a division of The Morehouse Group.

Cover design by Corey Kent of Morehouse Communications.

Library of Congress Cataloging-in-Publication Data

Stancliffe, Michael.
   Stars and angels : meditations for the Christian year / Michael Stancliffe.
       p.   cm.
   ISBN 0-8192-1736-0
   1. Church year meditations.   I. Title.
BV30.S64   1998
242'.3—dc21   97-31501
                                                        CIP

Printed in the United States of America

Acknowledgments
An extract from *Classical Landscape with Figures* by Osbert Lancaster
is reprinted by permission of John Murray (Publishers) Ltd.

Verses from 'Lord of the Dance' by Sydney Carter are copyright
© Stainer & Bell Ltd, and are reprinted by permission.

Extracts from *The Dark Labyrinth* by Lawrence Durrell
are reprinted by permission of Faber and Faber Ltd.

Extracts from 'East Coker' and 'The Dry Salvages' by T.S. Eliot are reprinted
from his *Four Quartets* by permission of Faber and Faber Ltd.

Contents

CONTENTS

Foreword

What makes a dead dean so special? Why are his sermons and meditations worth reprinting? These are questions which today's readers are entitled to ask on encountering this book, particularly if they are accustomed to seeing yards of unread volumes of sermons in theological libraries. But the dead dean is Michael Stancliffe, an outstanding Anglican of the twentieth century, and his best writings were not ephemeral in their topical relevance but timeless in their spiritual depth. Stancliffe, whose appointment to the Winchester Deanery in 1969 crowned a distinguished career, was also the disciple of another great twentieth-century preacher, Austin Farrer, and like Farrer his message is as arresting today as it was yesterday.

There are four qualities about this book which make it particularly attractive. First, it reflects the interaction of theology with the arts, most notably literature, painting and music. This is without question the work of a cultured, civilized all-rounder, a modern Renaissance Man. Second, the text is supremely readable. This is the work of a gifted writer, not a theological hack. Third, the atmosphere generated reflects the great hallmarks of Anglicanism; it is moderate, scholarly, humble and good-humoured. This is the work of a priest who was thoroughly grounded in the three-fold Anglican ethos of reason, scripture and tradition. And fourth, the book reveals a unique vision shot through and through with the glory of God and the wonder of creation. This is the work of a devout Christian who drew his strength from the daily office, in particular the Eucharist, and who was nurtured by a complex mixture of biblical and naturalistic images.

Not surprisingly Stancliffe champions the imaginative insights of the artist, the poet, the prophet and the mystic. Famous names burst on to the pages like cascades of shooting stars: Dante, Chaucer, Shakespeare, William Blake, George Herbert, Jane Austen, Thomas Hardy, T. S. Eliot, Lewis Carroll, Charles Williams, Lawrence Durrell – all have their part to play in

Stancliffe's fascinating and often very moving essays. The painting of Piero della Francesca, the architecture of Le Corbusier, the spiritual genius of Julian of Norwich, the importance of music, the beauty of gardens, the mystical significance of pilgrimages, the endless rhythms of the sea – no topic seems to escape either his artist's eye or his instinct to celebrate life in all its teeming variety.

But Stancliffe is never pretentious, and he has an essential appreciation of simplicity which is revealed whenever he writes of silence, solitude and beauty. My favourite piece in this collection is 'Seeing Stars'. I found this not only an exquisitely written essay on the splendour of the summer night-sky in Greece but also a most satisfying meditation on how hard it is for modern people, immersed in the bright, noisy busyness of life today, to perceive the dark immensity of God.

Sermons from Stancliffe's two books, *Jacob's Ladder* and *Symbols and Dances*, mingled with meditations written for the *Daily Telegraph* and with previously unpublished material, provide not only an outstanding series of writings to savour during the Christian year but a fitting memorial to Michael Stancliffe's uniquely gifted and creative Christian vision.

Susan Howatch

Introduction

It seems to me no accident that the Christian year and the natural year should have so much in common. Each frames the rhythms of life, and offers us the steps of a dance from life to death and from death to life in which we may place our stumbling feet and discover what God has in store for those who truly love him.

This pattern, this conjunction, was clearly one of those which had lodged deep in my father's mind, so that it was never possible to tell when he began to preach whether the world observed or the truth revealed would be his starting point. He was equally happy to begin a sermon with the geological analysis of the stone of which the particular church whose dedication festival was being celebrated was made, as with proclamation of the resurrection. As a result, there are few of his addresses and articles which do not move creatively between the two patterns which he saw as fundamental to a coherent view of the universe, and the place and purpose of human life within it. This is borne out by many of the themes around which he constructed successive series of articles for the Saturday edition of the *Daily Telegraph*. Gardens, the stars, the sea, hands, mazes, pilgrimage, bread, water – these and many more helped thousands to move from contemplating the natural order with its subtleties and variety to catching a glimpse of the divine activity, not just in creation, but in the redemption of the world and ultimate purpose of God for us all.

At the end of his life, he published a slim volume of sermons. *Symbols and Dances* had a characteristically punning title that alerted readers to the allusive, many layered, carefully crafted writing that was typical of the sermons that he produced week after week throughout his ministry, whether for a parish communion in Watermoor or the benchers of Lincoln's Inn, the pulpit of St Margaret's Westminster or a school speech-day. The readers of *Symbols and Dances* demanded more, and before he died he chose another collection of sermons which followed on its heels and was published as *Jacob's Ladder*.

Stars and Angels is a different venture. Rather than reprint as one volume those sermons which my father had already prepared for publication, it was decided to quarry the substantial amount of material he left – sermons and other devotional articles – for a book of a different kind. Here are sermons indeed – and nearly all of them have already appeared in *Symbols and Dances* or in *Jacob's Ladder*. But there are also a number of writings from the Saturday column of the *Daily Telegraph*, and the whole collection has been chosen and arranged to provide a companion to the Christian year.

The Christian year recalls the mighty acts of God in Christ, and celebrates them around two major foci – the incarnation and the redemption. Advent prepares for the coming of God among his people; this is particularized in the Nativity, and broadcast in the Epiphany. Only then does the story move to the journey of Lent, to the Passion, Holy Week and Easter, culminating in Pentecost. Without the incarnation, God's redemptive act in Christ would not have touched us; without the redemption, God's sharing our human nature would have been no more than an ineffectual gesture of solidarity: 'that which God did not assume, he did not redeem.' It is this engagement of God with us that we might be one with him that locks the twin poles of the Church's year in place, with their ambivalence as to where the new start is. This ambivalence is reflected in the way the book is arranged: starting with preparing for Advent it ends with the Fall, and the traditional Advent theme of the Last Things.

The natural year echoes this: is this the new start, the new birth, the moment when the days begin to lengthen again – that old celebration of midwinter, or is it when the spring breaks and the new shoots burst into blossom? The continuity of Christian experience as some drop out and new Christians are woven into the endless dance of the Church's prayer and praise is a theme which runs through all his writing: the dance of life has no moment of beginning and no end, so it is possible to pick up this collection at any place and dip into it.

While the pattern of the book will encourage readers to use it as a companion to the Christian year, giving a season by season, week by week commentary on our experience of God's action in our lives, it could well be used as a programme for a week's retreat, taking Advent to Epiphany, or Lent to Trinity, or Trinity to the Last Things as a way of entering more deeply into the mystery of God. Some of the series of shorter meditations – Pilgrimage, Gardens, The Sea, Seeing Stars – will provide material for a quiet day or a week's nourishment for those on 'holyday', and may well be the place to start for those who are coming to his writings for the first time.

Others again who are used to the weekly pattern of *Celebrating Common Prayer* may wish to let the rhythms of that Office shape their reading from *Stars and Angels*. In that pattern, Friday, Sunday and Monday rehearse the Passion, Resurrection and outpouring of the Spirit, while Tuesday, Wednesday and Thursday focus on Advent, Incarnation and Epiphany, and Saturday, the day in the tomb, is marked by the Last Things and our life with the saints. Within such a liturgical framework, the sequences of shorter meditations might well provide just what is needed for a pause at Midday prayer, when we need to be reminded of what God is doing in his world, and how he invites us to recognize, celebrate and co-operate with him in disclosing the signs of his kingly rule.

For that is what *Stars and Angels* does: it provides an opportunity for us to glimpse the activity of God in the everyday experiences and encounters of life, and offers us not only a way of understanding our place in God's good order, but also a means of becoming what he is calling us to be – saints on our journey to heaven. This book is a guidebook to that journey.

David Stancliffe
Bishop of Salisbury

October 1996

BEFORE ADVENT

Breakpoint is Growthpoint

WE all fall down – and if we know this and are human enough to cry for mercy, to breathe again and again *Kyrie Eleison*, the first mercy we are given is the blessing of hope, the mercy of realizing that, despite the appearances, more than fragments remain. Not all is to be lost. Indeed, greater things may well be beginning. If winter comes, can spring be far behind? Exhausted by the heat of the summer, dessicated and dusty, the leaf wrinkles and withers, and the stalk that ties it to the tree grows frail and brittle. There comes the moment when wind or frost – it may be only a puff of the one or a nip of the other – snap the tie. Attachment fails, all holds give, the stalk breaks off, and the leaf drops down and away. But at the very point of failure is a small and hitherto unnoticed bud with all its tight promise of new growth to come. So, too, fruit falls, is smashed, explodes – and thus frees its seed for life. As Jesus put it: 'Unless a grain of wheat fall into the earth and die it remains alone; but if it dies it bears much fruit' (John 12:24). Breakpoint is growthpoint. Lord, have mercy upon us, and incline our eyes to see this law.

It follows that the Fall is the season *par excellence* for making new beginnings. We can make a fresh start at any time – some do it at the end of the midwinter feast, the tax inspector does it in April. But more and more do it in autumn – Members of Parliament, and judges, and farmers, as well as undergraduates and school-children. The Jewish New Year starts at this season, and the Church now begins its reading of the Bible all over again and goes back to the Book of Genesis and the great theme of Creation. When there is a reinvigorating nip in the air, and Shelley's wild west wind is sweeping and cleaning the earth – this is no bad time for me to ask God to help me pull myself together and make a new beginning.

Looking into Things

BECAUSE the bath was nearly full some of the water slopped over when Archimedes stepped into it. Many people would have seen no more than a mess on the bathroom floor – and that is all the camera would have seen. But Archimedes saw more than that, saw deeper than that. He saw a law of physics of universal significance, a principle which is still true centuries after the mess has been mopped up.

Again, most of the influential inhabitants of Jerusalem in 701 BC saw a mess of another kind – the surrounding countryside devastated and their city itself besieged by the armies of Assyria. But because they were not men of vision they could not see why this should be so. Were they not God's people, and a very devout people, continually thronging the Temple, observing all the sabbaths and other appointed feasts, and punctiliously offering endless sacrifices? However, there was one man of vision among them, the prophet Isaiah. He saw all that the others saw – the enemy camps outside the walls and the full churches, so to call them, inside. But he also saw something else inside – proud self-sufficiency, bribery, corruption, graft, the oppression of the weak and the denial of justice to the poor. Further, because he was a man of vision, Isaiah saw a connection between all those things. Like Archimedes he saw a principle of universal significance in that mess in and around Jerusalem, a principle which is still true, namely, that when religion is only a matter of outward form and the moral law of Almighty God is denied or flouted, then things go ill. 'Where there is no vision, the people perish' (Proverbs 29:18).

Yet again, all that many saw in the house of Simon the leper at Bethany was a woman emptying a pot of extremely expensive ointment over a faith-healer from Galilee. It was an outrageous waste. The ointment might have been sold and the considerable proceeds given for the relief of human distress. But the two persons chiefly concerned saw very much more than that. She saw in him something very much more than a faith-healer from the provinces, just as he saw in her something very much more than an extravagant exhibitionist – and what they saw in each other is valued to this day.

There is much more in most things – and in most persons – than lies upon the surface or appears at first sight. We have considered just three examples, and further instances could be multiplied. Just think what Coleridge saw in the shooting of an albatross and what Blake saw in a grain of sand; what Botticelli saw in the legend of the birth of Venus and Handel saw in a verse of the book of Job; what Moses saw in a burning bush and what the author of the Book of Revelation saw in all manner of things. Above all, think what Jesus saw in, for instance, mustard-seed and wineskins, in a hold-up on the Jerusalem–Jericho road and in bridesmaids late for a wedding; in an unjust steward and in a good shepherd. In the Poets' Corner in the south transept of Westminster Abbey there stands the late Sir Jacob Epstein's bronze bust of William Blake – and if you go and look at Blake, you will find that he looks at you; more than that, he looks *into* you. Even more so did Jesus of Nazareth look at people and into people, so that he could see what others did not see, and know what others did not know, even about themselves. Being a person of vision he could see that Peter would deny him, that Judas would betray him, and that he himself would be put to death.

He saw this last with peculiar clarity, for it is commonly the fate of the person of vision and insight to be without honour in his own country and in his own day. The majority of those around him – shallow-sighted neighbours, literal-minded contemporaries – these have little use for the man or woman of vision, the artist, the poet, the prophet, the mystic. Unable to see as far as he does, they feel uncomfortable, they don't understand, they dismiss his vision as illusion and, injured in their pride, mock and satirize him and decry him as a fraud. Later, when they discover that he has seen through them, has seen in their hearts what they hoped was well-hidden, then they secretly fear him; they attempt to silence him, sometimes to destroy him. He who sees too far, and therefore knows too much, is best removed: 'Let him be crucified.'

But, 'Where there is no vision the people perish.' Those who despise or reject the imaginative insights of the artist, poet, prophet, or mystic, those who imagine that virtually the whole of truth lies on the surface and so fail to see things as they really are – such people are heading for disaster. Shallow sight has accounted for the collapse of many empires, as it has accounted for the break up of many individual human beings. A classic example is given in the opening chapters of the First Book of Samuel. The chief priest Eli was old, and his eyes had waxed dim; his sons, the young priests Hophni and Phinehas, were living on the fat of the sacrifices in vice and great luxury; men of vision there were none, and the people were simply in the dark. As the Bible puts it: 'The word of the Lord was precious in those days; there was no open vision.' In such circumstances no one could see things as they really were. And then the Philistines came. In the opening battle the Israelite vanguard was routed, and in their blindness the people hurriedly fetched the Ark and rushed with this fetish into battle, shouting a great shout so that the earth rang again. The Philistines guessed what that shout meant, redoubled their efforts, captured the Ark, and easily overran the country. A secret weapon and a lot of patriotic shouting cannot save a people who have not been taught to look beyond the ends of their noses, or to recognize the existence of such invisible qualities as truth, integrity and righteousness. It was because there was someone of vision, Isaiah, in Jerusalem in 701 BC, and because the people on that occasion gave heed to his message that the siege was withstood and the enemy forced to withdraw. But where there is no vision the people perish.

And for three reasons: first, if we have no vision, and all the truth we recognize is what lies on the surface, then we shall perhaps be successful materialists, and we shall survive as long as we do not come up against someone with more brute strength, slick wits and animal cunning than ourselves. But if we have no vision we remain ignorant of all but a fraction of the truth, ignorant of most things as they really are, ignorant of all that the camera cannot see; ignorant, therefore, amongst other things, of God himself. And that, in the end, means that we perish.

But secondly, if we have no vision, such truth as we can see we see distorted and out of focus, out of proportion. We treat what is but a part as the whole, what is relative as absolute. So shallow sight means also a literal mind, and we rush an ark into battle, or an isolated text into debate, fondly but falsely imagining that we have the invincible power of truth on our side. And that in the end also means defeat.

And thirdly, if we have only shallow sight we shall have only a hard heart, for a narrow mind means a narrow sympathy. The scribes and Pharisees of Christ's day knew what they knew exceeding well. They had their scriptural texts by heart, and by them they ruled their own lives and the lives of others with an iron rigidity. They knew, they thought, exactly where they were and what was what − and accordingly crucified Jesus who didn't fit into their tidy little pattern. But what are those scribes and Pharisees now but monuments to the truth of Paul's words: 'The letter killeth; it is the spirit that giveth life'? Where there is no vision the people perish.

But who has this vision, this power of insight into things as they really are? Not everyone certainly − or rather, some have it to a markedly greater degree than others − the artist, the poet, the prophet, the mystic. A wise people honours such men and women and pays attention to them − even though it finds them hard to understand and their message often distasteful. But how do we know they are telling the truth? May they not be frauds? Yes, some of them may be − and there were false prophets in Old Testament times. But the false prophet can usually be detected by the bigness of his boasts and by the popularity of his promises. The genuine prophet, however, is a person of great humility, and is not ashamed to confess that he does not know everything. And the genuine prophet often has unpleasant things to say; he says what he has seen to be the truth, and not what he thinks will please the majority. Only the false prophet will claim that all is easier than it seems, that everyone is an angel, that there is nothing on earth to be afraid of, and certainly nothing in heaven to be afraid of.

Honour the man of vision then, and pay serious attention to what he says. But also, strive to become persons of keen insight yourselves. We are not most of us great visionaries, we can't all be an Archimedes, an Isaiah, a Blake. At the same time most of us can learn to see more than a camera does. A camera, they say, is dead accurate; but as Cecil Day Lewis remarked, what is the use of accuracy if it is dead? Start by expecting to see in things and in persons more than meets the eye. Do not be dazzled by surface glitter nor dismayed by apparent dullness. Do not be led astray by catchy sounds on the one hand, nor by ugly sounds on the other. Do not be satisfied with clichés, and always beware of the sin of taking things too literally – the letter killeth; it is the spirit that giveth life. So seek the help and inspiration of the Holy Spirit, who spake by the prophets, and part of whose work it is to lead us into all truth. Have the patience and discrimination to look *into* things, not just at them. Above all, and again and again, look not at, but into, Jesus – into what he said, into what he did, into what he is.

As the coming season of Advent reminds us, this is ultimately a matter of life and death. For where there is no vision the people perish.

Stir Up

SEE with the eyes of that part of your spirit which appreciates a work of art, together with the eyes of that part of you which should be aware of your cultural roots, a sheet of vellum on which an inscription has just been written. The ink is still wet, but the light of this winter afternoon is already fading and the work must stop. And anyhow a bell is ringing and the monk must leave the scriptorium and take himself off to chapel for Nones – leaving us the opportunity to study what he's been up to. The sheet on the desk is part of a book being made for the altar of the great Palatine Church just built for Charlemagne at Aachen at the turn of the eighth/ninth centuries.

Familiar as we are with newsprint and typescript we can't read fast enough; there's nothing in the characters themselves of newsprint and typescript to arrest our eye. But the text before us now is of a very different quality. Every character has character – as have all things that are handmade – and not least the large decorative E with which the inscription begins. After that capital E an X, C, I, T – which suggest 'excitement' is to come. But this first word ends abruptly with an A, for this is Latin in front of us. The whole text runs as follows:

Excita, quaesumus domine, tuorum fidelium voluntates: ut divini operis fructum propensius exequentes, pietatis tuae remedia maiora percipiant. Per dominum.

It stops there. The priests would know the usual formula with which to end the prayer, and in any case the light was going and the bell was ringing.

The translation you know: it is the collect for the Sunday before Advent:

Stir up, we beseech thee, O Lord, the wills of thy faithful people: that they, plenteously bringing forth the fruit of good works, may of thee be plenteously rewarded.

7

There is a considerable puzzle there – but leave that for the moment. It is with the stirring start that we must first concern ourselves. *Stir up, we beseech thee* – still the annual signal to good Anglican cooks to put the ingredients of the Christmas pudding into a bowl and to call every member of the household to come and lend a hand with the stirring. But it is not of pudding but of ourselves that the collect speaks; it is we who are to be stirred, and God who is asked to do the stirring. So we had best keep mum if we are satisfied with things as they are, with ourselves as we are. It is *we* who are to be stirred – and God who is prayed, almost commanded, to do the stirring. That is one of the arresting features of this collect; in most prayers God's name comes first – 'Our Father' or 'Almighty God', but this starts with two imperative monosyllables in English, *Stir up* – in Latin, *Excita* – literally, make to move and agitate an inert and stodgy mass, our *wills*. Our bodies are lazy enough when it comes to doing the things we ought to be doing; our intellects and imaginations can go quietly through a week without being unduly exercised about anything apart from what concerns our material well-being. But the will is the laziest of all our members – and not least at this time of year. All is on the ebb. It is the fall. Summer's heat has drained away and all its petals dropped. Autumn is sinking deeper into winter, the year is waning, life fading. Everything is running down. The clouds return after the rain, the doors are shut in the streets, desire fails, man goeth to his long home and the mourners go about the streets. Or ever the silver cord be loosed, or the golden bowl be *broken*, or the pitcher be *broken* at the fountain, or the wheel *broken* at the cistern. Then shall the dust return to the earth as it was (cf. Ecclesiastes 3:3–7). At such a season, in such a mood, the will is weakest, our self-starter most unreliable and prone to fail. Therefore: *Stir up, O Lord, the wills of thy faithful people.*

Of thy faithful people – not of mankind at large. No doubt the wills of all people need stirring, and we could all make a list of individuals whose wills we should be glad to see stirred into action. Maybe – but what we ask in this prayer is that the Church should be shaken up and ourselves stirred. It is easy to feel established and comfortably settled if we come regularly to church, say our prayers, and help lame dogs over stiles on the rare occasions when we come to a stile and happen to meet there a dog – and the dog lame. But Christians are called to do a lot more than that!

So much for the stirring start to this collect. Now the puzzle. Our perplexity is this: the reason given for praying that our wills be stirred up is so that, plenteously bringing forth the fruit of good works, we may of God be plenteously rewarded. Are you content that your Christian living should be inspired by that profit motive? Are you happy to accept the suggestion that the overriding purpose of your life should be this: to be so prolific in your good works to God and neighbour that you may earn a bumper crop of advantages for yourself?

It is true that Jesus plainly spoke of rewards for those who follow him faithfully. But he also made it clear that he who seeks to save his life shall lose it. Remembering that, remembering too that 'charity seeketh not her own', how can we deliberately pray that we may be stirred to live in such a way that we may be paid top prices for our crop of good works?

It is a fact that the Latin collect with which we began, which had been used throughout Western Europe on the Sunday next before Advent every year since the time of Charlemagne, suffered enormous violence when it was translated into English by Cranmer and his liturgical commission for our *Book of Common Prayer*. What the motive was cannot be known with any certainty. What is certain is that when Cranmer englished this collect he translated the first half with strict accuracy, the second half with no accuracy at all. It is almost the kind of work for which a pupil would be sent to the head. Literally translated the original would run: 'Stir up, we beseech, O Lord, the wills of thy faithful people, that they, seeking more readily the fruit of the divine work, may come to possess the greater remedies of thy piety.'

Which makes a deal of a difference. We should be asking that we may be stirred up to *seek* fruits rather than grow them, fruits of *God's* producing, not of our own; fruits of his divine work, all the blessings he has made available to us through the life, death and resurrection of Jesus Christ. And we are to seek these blessings not that we may have plentiful rewards, but rather that we may be given great *remedies* – not prizes for our perfection, but pills and prescriptions for our imperfections.

And that puts an entirely different complexion upon things, and the aptness of this collect to our present condition becomes plain indeed. All things may not be running down so literally or so fast as the writer of Ecclesiastes felt, but they are drawing towards an end. The old year is passing and next Sunday a new year begins for Christians, with Advent reminding them not only to prepare to celebrate at Christmas Christ's first coming to save us, but also to prepare us for his second coming to judge us. Next Sunday's collect tells us that it is high time to awake out of sleep, the night being far spent and the day at hand. This week the collect should begin to get us moving. Summer's petals are all dropped, the light of the winter afternoon is fast fading, and a bell is ringing. We must go to prayers.

ADVENT

Thank God for Darkness

WHATEVER may one day be discovered in Loch Ness, all that a group of biologists could find at the bottom a few years ago were three worms, three crustaceans and one mollusc – for the Loch is 750 feet deep and therefore its bed is totally dark. Light is well nigh essential to life, while darkness spells nothingness and death – which is why, almost throughout the Bible, light symbolizes the nature and activity of God and darkness stands for that which is chaotic and evil. So in the collect for Advent, and picking up the words of Paul (Romans 13:12), we pray for grace to cast away the works of darkness and put upon us the armour of light.

But is all darkness bad? Isn't there something to be said in praise of it? There is – and the Bible says it. In the first place, in a world of work and weariness the darkness of night is a great blessing at the end of a day's labours (Psalm 104:20, 23–4). It soothes and refreshes us, helps us to rest, and obliterates for a few hours what we are glad to be able to forget for a while. But secondly, the Hebrews could sometimes think of God being *within* darkness. Certainly he is light, and in him is no darkness at all (1 John 1:5); but around and about him there is deep shadow (Psalm 18:11) and Isaiah could exclaim: 'Verily thou art a God that hidest thyself' (Isaiah 45:15).

This darkness represents the idea that in his full being, in all his ineffable goodness and power, God is utterly beyond the comprehension of sinful mortals. As we now are we may, if we will, see God indirectly – reflected in the wonders of the universe, in all sights and sounds of beauty, and in the lives of lovely people. But as mortals we cannot see him direct, nor comprehend him in all his dazzling intensity. It is our hope that hereafter we shall see him face to face, but now we only see through a glass darkly (1 Corinthians 13:12). We should repeatedly thank him for the blessing of night and for that merciful darkness which protects us from more than we could stand.

Hearing Aids

GENERATIONS of men and women have found it a true re-creation to hear, read, mark, learn and inwardly digest a few verses of the Bible first thing every morning – to muse on them, let their imaginations play round them, and allow their minds to feed on them in the simple belief that as they do so God will somehow communicate with them and speak to them through the medium of the words on which they thus meditate. They have said that through their doing this the Holy Spirit has undoubtedly shaped and inspired them and made something new of them – and that is true re-creation.

But perhaps it does not seem to 'work' in our case. If that is so, then it is time we asked some questions. And the person above all from whom we should demand an explanation is God himself. We should not be shy or afraid to challenge him with some very straight and pointed questions: What on earth do you mean? What are you getting at and trying to show me through these words I am pondering? What are you telling me to *do* today? – and for whom? What are you suggesting I should *say* today? – and to whom? Or what are you saying I should *be* today?

Provided we give the time for the replies to be received – and a few minutes of attentive and sensitive thinking are certainly required – the answers to one or more of those questions will usually be given. If they are not, or if they are not clear, I shall be unwise to jump to the conclusion that it is God's fault. All the chances are that the failure of communication is due to one of three causes in myself. It may be that I simply cannot make head or tail of the meaning of the actual words in front of me (though this should be rare when we are reading a Gospel), in which case a modern translation will probably help. Or, secondly, I am a good deal thicker and deafer this morning than I realize. What sort of a night have I had? And what sort of attention should I pay anybody else just now – unless he or she shouted at me? But God does not appear to like raising his voice at us, and it was C. S. Lewis who said that when God shouts at us it is in our pains.

The third and probably commonest reason why I don't hear God is that I don't like what he says. The answers to the questions are all too plain – but thoroughly unpalatable. I cannot swallow them, let alone stomach them. They will give me a pain in my pride and upset my own ideas and plans for what I want to do and say and be today.

A Time to Keep Silence

'Geoffrey Day is a clever man if ever there was one. Never says anything; not he.'

'Never.'

'You might live wi' that man, my sonnies, a hundred years, and never know there was anything in him.'

'Ay; one o' these up-country London ink-bottle chaps would call Geoffrey a fool.'

'Ye never find out what's in that man: never,' said Spinks. 'Close? ah, he is close! He can hold his tongue well. That man's dumbness is wonderful to listen to.'

'There's so much sense in it. Every moment of it is brimmen over wi' sound understanding.'

That's how my text of *Under the Greenwood Tree* runs. But there seems to be a variant reading which, while not altering the sense, states it more strikingly:

'Silent? ah, he is silent! He can keep silence well. That man's silence is wonderful to listen to.'

'There's so much sense in it. Every moment of it is brimmen over with sound understanding.'

Not all silence is so full and deep and sensitive. Not all silence is golden. There is the leaden silence of a vacuum, the dead silence of a tomb, the empty silence of an uninhabited desert. There is a silence which is the carapace of the shy, the virtue of fools, the refuge of cowards, the shell of the lazy, the castle of the self-sufficient egoist. But in the main, silence is divine, it is golden; it is full and deep and sensitive, almost alive and certainly powerful. And we shall the better estimate its quality and power by reflecting upon the disintegration and destruction which so often follow upon its absence. For sound, the breaking of silence, can (and often does) break much else besides. Trumpets and shouts destroyed Jericho; a musical note of a particular frequency will

15

shiver a goblet to splinters; aircraft breaking the sound-barrier can smash an acre of glasshouses. If we happen to live and try to sleep within a mile or two of a major airport we do not need to be reminded of the destructive power of sound; and, for all of us, the sudden squeal of the brakes of a car or the rasping screech of a mechanical saw can shiver our spines; while the various drills which bore into our roadways and our teeth seem to threaten to pierce and split our brains, to disintegrate our very beings. How much the sheer noise of twentieth-century life is contributing to the increasing destruction of our mental health I do not know – but pandemonium is totally devilish. It is the very opposite of silence; it is the din of hell.

Nor are our machines the worst offenders. It is the sounds made by our own mouths which do most damage to individuals and to communities. Recall what brought to an end the association of those who were building the Tower of Babel. Recall the sounds which persuaded Pilate to order the crucifixion of Jesus. Recall the voice of Hitler and the destruction which *that* did.

Nor does someone have to be a Hitler for their words to be destructive of human relationships. Obvious enough is the hurt done by gossips and backbiters, by controversialists with a gift for spite, critics with a taste for cruelty. But equally damaging to human relationships and human society can be the monotonous rumbling of bores, the chatter of birdwits, the grumbling of the discontented, the bragging of the boasters, the silky speech of the seducers and, by no means least, the preaching of the improvers.

The preaching of the improvers – and that means (or should mean) most of us, Christians and Humanists, clergy and laity alike, reformers of every kind. We all wish – or ought to wish – to help others to become happier and healthier and finer than they are; and as Christians we believe that, with God's help, we have the power to do so and the duty to do so. We have a 'mission' to them, as we know – and it is part of that mission to go into all the world and preach the gospel to every creature. We wish for them to have what we have been given, and to become as fortunate as we are. And so we address ourselves to them; we break silence and speak to them. We argue with them as honestly as we can; we try to prove, in all sincerity, that some of their beliefs are untrue or their practices wrong; we try to demonstrate, in all humility, why we think *our* beliefs are true and *our* practices right; and we seek to persuade them to give up being what they are that they may become like us and share our good fortune. We do not mean to assert ourselves. We do not consciously set ourselves over against them, still less do we intentionally set ourselves above them. But that is what it comes to. That is what it often looks like to them. And (is it not so?) again and again the result is the opposite of what we hoped for, and our speech is destructive of understanding between us. For those we thus address feel that they are being talked at, got at, indoctrinated; their resistance is aroused, their defences go up. They resent what appears to them as our arrogance; they resent our assertiveness, which appears to them as an interference with their human integrity. They resent, too, the fact that, while we expect them to take us seriously and to listen to us, we do not always appear to take them so seriously or to be really prepared to listen to them.

And that is where we go wrong. We speak so much in our desire that they may be happier and finer and that they may share what we so richly enjoy. But we do not allow a place for silence, we do not know the strength of silence and we have no faith in the power of silence. We do not understand that, as George Meredith put it, 'speech is the small change of silence'. We often teach and preach about the teaching and preaching of Jesus and are adept at spinning out ten plain words of his into two thousand of our own. But we do not sufficiently often think upon the silences of Jesus – his thirty years of silence before he ever began to preach; his silence in wilderness and on mountainside; in particular his silence before his accusers and how he held his peace when he hung upon the cross while the noisy revolutionaries, as is the way of revolutionaries, made rings round him and yelled their heads off at him. We wish to be, in the best and fullest sense of the word, the friends of those whom we long to save and 'convert' – but we have not grasped what is the greatest office of a friend: to lay down our lives for them, to put ourselves on one side for their sake.

Now I am not saying that there is no place for preaching – I should hardly be here if I believed that. I'm not saying we should not each of us speak to persuade others to accept what we honestly believe to be the truth. What I am saying is that before the speaking there must be silence, and that what we say, and how we say it, will come out of what we have learned in the silence about God, about ourselves, and about those whom we are trying to help. It is the silence – maybe short, maybe long, maybe half a minute, maybe half an hour, maybe half a lifetime – it is the silence that will create the conditions and the opportunity for us to speak, as it is in the silence that we shall be shown what we ought to say and how to say it.

We cannot too often reflect upon the creative power of silence, and we cannot too strongly emphasize the importance of our possessing ourselves in humility and patience to let the silence work. 'We know' (it has been said) 'that serious things have to be done in silence, because we do not have words to measure the immeasurable. In silence we love, pray, listen, compose, paint, write, think, suffer. These experiences are all occasions of giving and receiving, of some encounter with forces that are inexhaustible and independent of us. These are as easily distinguishable from our routines and possessiveness as silence is distinct from noise.'

What does this silence of which I am speaking require of us? Two things at least:

First: it means bringing ourselves in silence into the presence of God, jabbering much less to him, listening much more. It means becoming more sensitive to him, more open to him and to his inspiration. In this way, in such silence, we come to know him better – and, in consequence, to know ourselves better by contrast, to recognize more clearly our limitations, our own need of help and that we ourselves are very far from being perfect.

Secondly: being silent, cultivating that kind of silence which Geoffrey Day had, that silence which was so wonderful to listen to and which was brimming over with understanding – such silence involves a deliberate refusal to assert ourselves and to get at others; it involves putting ourselves alongside them, and as far as possible into their hearts and minds; coming to understand, as fully and as truthfully as we can, how the world looks to them, how we look to them, how God looks to them; why they believe as they do and behave as they do; it involves recognizing that they are human as we are human, that they too are made in the image of God, that in them too is something of the divine, something of the light that lighteth every man coming into the world. It involves so learning to respect them that we give up all thought of possessing them, of manipulating them, of indoctrinating them, of persuading them to cease to be themselves and to become facsimiles of ourselves. It involves holding ourselves in silent readiness to speak only when the time comes. The time will come, when, because they have learnt to trust us and respect us and recognize how much we care about them, they ask us to break silence, to speak, to tell them the secret of our patience with them and of our compassion for them. Certainly we have a mission to mankind. But it should always start from silence, and it should never become noisy. 'Be swift to hear, slow to speak' (James 1:19). 'For everything there is a season, and a time for every matter under the sun – a time to keep silence, and a time to speak' (Ecclesiastes 3:1, 7).

Joy and Generosity

ECAUSE the Lord is at hand we should rejoice and let our moderation be obvious – at least, that is what, in the language of the AV, Paul told the Philippians (14:4–5). But neither rejoicing nor moderation are now understood as Paul understood them. Christian joy has little in common with that loud, hearty happiness induced by turkey and alcohol in the stomach and a paper hat on the head, and resulting in a fumey feeling that we are jolly good fellows – and a fumey forgetfulness of the dark outside. Christian joy springs rather from the realization that, in spite of what we secretly know ourselves to be, God still cares for us and will come to us and be with us. And because of that, and because God once came to a cowshed, we cannot be ignorant or forgetful of what goes on in the darkness and what it means to be outside. Our joy is of the kind that comes near to tears, and is grounded in the profound sense of relief that comes of knowing that we still matter to God and that he is ready to come to us – outside and in the dark as we are.

And then the Christian is to be moderate. Today this implies little more than temperance, control, avoiding extremes. But Paul's word was much richer in meaning and included gentleness, understanding and forebearance. It is translated 'magnanimity' in the NEB. It is a wide generosity, the very opposite of every kind of small-mindedness, legal quibbling, or tight totting-up of what I am owed. It is the disposition of those who don't stand on their rights, or insist that because somebody else has this and that, therefore they are entitled to this and that too; of those who treat others with limitless understanding, recognizing that there must be give and take if we are to live together as God intends – and who are therefore ready to do rather more than their fair share of giving and rather less than their fair share of taking. In fact, people of Christian moderation would not use those words. They are not particularly interested in whether their own share of the world's goods is fair. They have the priceless gift of knowing that the Lord is at hand – for all, and even for themselves.

CHRISTMAS EVE

Great Little One

ONE of the most attractive features of the Christmas story is the fact that, to all outward appearances, it is concerned with small things. At the heart of it is a human being at its smallest, and that newborn child is surrounded by no greatness – no palace, no pomp, no grand people – but lies in a simple manger in a plain stable and between two peasants. Nor had the first to join that little group anything impressive about them – shepherds on night duty don't look princely – and it was only later that more imposing personages put in an appearance. Christians believe that what happened in that small setting was of cosmic significance, and something of that significance is expressed by St John in the prologue to his Gospel. But it is not apparent at the outset. We begin with a little tiny child in a small place, and it is that which first attracts rather than St John's statement that 'the Word was made flesh'.

What is the reason for this? Is it just sentimentality? That is arguable and in certain cases possibly true: there are some people who get an emotional kick out of cuddly things and talking baby talk to little darlings. But a much more obvious and common reason is the fact that Luke's picture of the birth in the stable is altogether more straightforward and comprehensible than John's theological definition. We can grasp the meaning of what we can visualize – a baby in a manger – much more easily than the meaning of such an abstract concept as 'the Word made flesh', particularly if we've heard tell that 'Word' and 'flesh' in that phrase mean rather more than they mean in our everyday speech.

But, more fundamentally, it is worth considering whether there is not something inherently attractive in *smallness*. It has nothing whatever to do with sentimentality, but simply that 'small is beautiful'. The social anthropologist Lévi–Strauss, in the opening chapter of *The Savage Mind*, digresses from his examination of the nature and function of myth to ask why it is that so many of us are fascinated and delighted by small-scale models – from dolls' houses and Dinky toys, ships in bottles and Japanese gardens up to the illuminations in medieval manuscripts, the miniatures of a Holbein or Hilliard and the paintings of those Dutch and Flemish artists who delighted to paint such tiny details in their pictures that they must have used a magnifying glass to paint them as we need one to see them. Lévi-Strauss goes on to suggest that the small-scale model or miniature is the universal type of the work of art; that all miniatures seem to have an intrinsic aesthetic quality (and whence do they derive that virtue if not from the dimensions themselves?); and that the vast majority of works of art are in fact small-scale, reductions from life-size. And it isn't just a question of economy in the use of materials or the inconvenience of having to house objects that are as large as life. There appears to be some inherent virtue in reduction itself. Small is beautiful. A small-scale model enables a person contemplating it to acquire straight away some understanding of the object represented *in its totality*, and of how it is related to everything else. If we want to understand a thing, the usual procedure is to take it to bits. We divide to conquer; we analyse to understand – and we inevitably lose something in the process, for a whole is greater than the sum of its parts and cannot be fully appreciated if isolated from everything else. But in a miniature or model we have the whole; small it is and much reduced in size, but we can grasp it as a whole from the outset, and we are left to work up to full-scale as and when we can, free to meditate upon it and to use our imagination to enlarge it until it embraces (as it may if it has been truly and faithfully made) not only the original large as life but much else besides – for such a model can have infinite relations.

For example: the novels of Jane Austen are miniatures; she herself described them as such when she wrote of 'the little bit (two inches wide) of Ivory on which I work with so fine a brush'. Each of her novels is a small-scale model: the details are minute and perfect and the subject confined to very narrow limits – 'human nature in the midland counties' she once called it. In her lifetime the French Revolution happened, the Napoleonic Wars were fought and the Industrial Revolution progressed at an accelerating speed until it was come to the dawn of the Railway Age. But her novels are without reference to these turbulent happenings. However, as Lord David Cecil has pointed out, in those novels she 'presented the struggle that was rending intellectual Europe. On her bit of ivory she has engraved a criticism of life as serious and as considered as Hardy's'. Thus we can see in them not only a picture of all Europe in 1815 but also a picture of all the world in the later twentieth century.

In a similar way William Blake saw (and helps us to see) the world in a grain of sand and heaven in a wild flower; Julian of Norwich saw the cosmos in a hazelnut; and St John saw all that he saw in the child born in the stable – the Word that was in the beginning with God, and was God; the Word by whom all things were made, and in whom was life, and that life the light of men.

And as we meditate along these lines we realize that it is chiefly through miniatures and models that most of us come to possess what we have of eternal truth. What else, for instance, are the parables of Jesus but 'little bits of ivory two inches wide worked on with a fine brush'? They are brilliant little pictures, drawn within tiny limits and made up of small matters – sheep and goats, a sower in a field, a traveller coming on a man who had been mugged, a grain of mustard seed. But such miniatures are seen to have infinite relations when pondered by those who make the time to give them more than a passing glance, whose wit is to be well read in simplicity, and who know that things are not to be judged by outward appearance nor despised because they are small. For nearly two thousand years those with such an outlook have been haunted by the inherent beauty of the little Bethlehem scene and come to know and love God through it. Small is beautiful, and we still delight to welcome the 'great little one'. The phrase comes from Crashaw's *An Hymn of the Nativity, Sung as by the Shepherds*, and the poem is worth musing upon as an English poet's version of St John's prologue:

Welcome all wonders in one sight!
   Eternity shut in a span,
Summer in winter, day in night,
   Heaven in earth and God in Man;
Great little one! whose all embracing birth
Lifts earth to heaven, stoops heaven to earth.

Welcome! though not to those gay flies
   Gilded in the beams of earthly kings,
Slippery souls in smiling eyes,
   But to poor shepherds, home-spun things,
Whose wealth's their flock, whose wit to be
Well read in their simplicity.

CHRISTMAS DAY

A Meditation for Christmas

THE more serious and sensitive among us are not always so comfortable in our minds at Christmas as our outward behaviour might suggest. In our more serious moments we are aware of, and embarrassed by, a sharp and painful contrast between the event we are celebrating and the world in which we are celebrating it.

The event is dangerously familiar – the birth of a particular child some twenty centuries ago. Thanks to the work of generations of artists and the pictures on the Christmas cards, we know the scene backwards – a stable, simple indeed, but clean and homely; well lit and apparently warm, for Joseph wears no overcoat and the shepherds no mufflers. Admittedly there is something incongruous in the presence of the ox and ass – but then, what a mild-eyed ox and what a docile donkey. In the centre the smiling infant lies comfortably in a bed so soft and sweet that, in some pictures, the manger looks more like a cradle than a cattle trough. It is all very peaceful and beautiful.

And this is where our embarrassment begins, for what has that scene to do with the world in which it is our lot to·live? It seems utterly remote from our world of political and industrial strife; of racial and sectarian hatred; of material greed and reckless exploitation of the earth's dwindling resources; of unemployment and homelessness and hunger. Has the event we are celebrating and which the artists have commemorated anything meaningful and relevant for those who live in an age of money, steel, concrete, chemicals, splintered atoms and deadly rays? Is it anything more than a sentimental picture to which we cling as an excuse for a few days' escape from the gaunt reality of the deep midwinter's gloom? Did this thing we think we are celebrating really happen, or is it only a fairy tale for men and women who haven't grown up?

The whole corpus of documents which together make up the New Testament gives an unequivocal answer to such questions. Each book in its own way asserts that the event now celebrated is no fairy story but the most important event in history, the birth of God in human form; and that if, and when, the significance of that event is appreciated it does to people now what it did to shepherds then – it knocks them down on their knees in wonder and reverence and then lifts them up again and sends them on their way singing in hope and joy.

And if we find that hard to believe – as many not unnaturally do, for our atmosphere of murk and fume is poison to the finer apprehensions of the human spirit – then perhaps the picture on the Christmas card is largely responsible. For it is no literal likeness of the historical event, as a few minutes' meditation on the Gospel story will make clear. There is nothing in the New Testament to suggest that the actual birth of Jesus Christ was in any way miraculous or abnormal. Any miracle happened nine months earlier. But the birth itself, so far as we know, was just like any other birth, with labour and travail and sharp pains – and no anaesthetics. Moreover, as Luke's story plainly says, it all happened in far from comfortable surroundings – in an outhouse, there being no room in the inn. The shepherds did not find the baby in a cosy cot in a private ward of a maternity hospital, nor even in a rough cradle in a peasant's cottage, but in a cattle trough in a cattle shed. And whatever cattle sheds may be today they were not particularly dry, warm or hygienic places twenty centuries ago. They were places of dirt and dung and mud, spiders and beetles and bugs, with the straw on the floor smelly and sodden. If there was a lamp it flickered fitfully in the draughts. And then there were sizeable brutes – no cuddly bunnies or Christmassy robins but a bull in one corner and a donkey in another. 'There is born to you a saviour,' the angel told the shepherds – yes, but with pain and tears in a dirty, draughty, ill-lit outhouse, and with beasts for company. The world on which Jesus first opened his eyes was no tinsel-pretty nursery, but the dim interior of a sordid shed.

We begin to recognize the place. It is our own familiar world in miniature, a world that we know only too well to be dirty, draughty, ill-lit and a stamping ground of brutes. It is soiled with all the greed and stupidity of man, draughty with cold currents of fear and suspicion, and so dark that its peoples stumble from puddle to puddle since they have no light strong and steady enough to show them the ways of peace. And then there are the beasts – some hell-bent on throwing their weight about and indulging their passions, others idiotic and obstinate in their self-ishness and petty pride. The environment with which we are all too familiar is precisely the kind of environment into which Jesus was born; not a world in which all is order and beauty, but one of sin and suffering and fearful power. And he came into it then, and he can come into it today where it will have him, to save it and give it peace.

But the stable is more. It is also the human heart writ large, for that heart is spoiled and soiled with thoughts and imaginings to which one would generally blush to own; windy with fear and cold with envy; ill-lit too, for the lantern of conscience cannot burn bright and steady in such draughts. And the beasts in the human heart are boringly familiar – greed, pride, lust and obsti-nacy among the most brutish of them. It was to people with hearts like this (and not wholly unlike our own, we have to admit) that Jesus came – and comes today if we will have him.

But what will happen then? Suppose we allow him to be born in ourselves and to live and grow and rule in us – what then? Dare we? 'Be not afraid,' said the angel, 'I bring you good tidings of great joy.' And if we look again at the traditional Christmas card and nativity scene we are shown what does indeed happen when God is allowed to enter the lives and affairs of us humans. The dirt disappears, the cold is banished, light streams in, and the beasts fall to their knees. The artists, as usual, are right after all. It is the witness of the whole of the New Testament that these were the effects of the coming of Jesus Christ to men and women, and it can happen – and does happen – in ourselves and in our world today if we will have it so.

But the courtesy of God, like the patience of God, is infinite. Unlike some of his more fanatical servants, God will not impose himself nor force an entrance where he is not wanted. It may be that we fear the consequences to ourselves, to our habitual ways of thinking and our cherished standards of living, if we were to admit him. But don't be afraid, says the angel. I've got news of great joy for you. If you don't pay attention then you will indeed continue to live in fear – and with reason. But if you do attend, then the news I bring you will do to you what it did to those shepherds who heard it first. It will send you on a voyage of discovery. And if you have the will to complete that journey you will find yourself brought to your knees in wonder and reverence – and then lifted up and sent on your way singing.

God Rest You Merry, Gentlemen

God rest you merry, gentlemen,
Let nothing you dismay

— and, as a contribution both to your merriment and to the defeat of dismay, here is a story. It's not a short story, and those who already know and love it must forgive my ruthless and prosaic abbreviation of it. And if it seems to have not much to do with Bethlehem or with our own situation in the midwinter of 1982 — well, Christmas is traditionally a time for games and puzzles, and if you need a solution to this puzzle you will find it at the end. Are you sitting comfortably? Then I'll begin.

Once upon a time, in Winchester, some think, a King called Arthur and his court were celebrating Christmas with all its medieval richness — twelve days of merriment to defeat that deep depression induced by all the cold and dark of midwinter in Northern Europe. There was churchgoing, feasting, carols and dancing, exchange of presents, telling of stories, playing of games. And on New Year's Day, just as dinner was beginning, something happened which instantly hushed the whole merry company. There rode into the Great Hall a man on horseback, a man whose clothes, skin, hair, even his horse, were all bright green. In one hand he held a bunch of holly, in the other a whacking great axe. 'I've heard of your reputation for honour, courage, and courtesy,' said the Green Man, 'and I offer you a Christmas game. Let's see how brave and good you are. Let one of you take this axe and cut off my head. There's only one rule in the game. It's this: the man with the courage to take up this challenge must meet me a year from now and allow me to do to him what he now does to me.'

'What foolery,' said the King. 'Then you are afraid!' 'Not at all,' replied the King somewhat nettled, and rose to accept the challenge. 'It's wrong for the King's life to be risked,' said Sir Gawain,

Preached in Winchester Cathedral on Christmas Day 1982.

'let me do it.' All agreed that it was proper he should take the King's place. The Green Man dismounted, gave Gawain the axe, bent his head, bared his neck, and said 'Strike.' Gawain struck – and the head went rolling over the floor and among the feet of the lords and ladies at table. The Green Man fetched his head, gathered it into his arms and, speaking through its mouth, said: 'Right. Now keep your word. Meet me in a year's time in the Green Chapel.' And with that he mounted, rode out of the Hall, and disappeared.

So much for a bald summary of the start of this strange story, that poem called *Sir Gawain and the Green Knight* – a poem which is, in its own way, as great a work of art and superb craftsmanship as this nave in which we are gathered. William of Wykeham was building this here at exactly the same time as an unknown poet in north-west England was constructing, in celebration of Christmas, the poem of which I am reminding you.

To resume its story: when the Green Man had left the Hall, Arthur and his company resumed their merriment. They let nothing them dismay. And when the twelve days of Christmas were over life returned to normal and the seasons came and went until, in autumn at All Saints' Tide, Gawain with growing foreboding said goodbye to his companions, and rode out alone in search of the Green Chapel where honour required him to be in two months' time. The journey was long and hard; it was a cold coming he had of it in the bleak midwinter of north-west England. And time was running short when, on Christmas Day, he chanced upon a fine castle and asked for lodging. He was most warmly welcomed and invited to join the Christmas house party in the castle. Gawain was merry and let nothing him dismay, for the lord of the castle said that the Green Chapel about which Gawain asked was only a couple of miles away. 'After your long hard journey you need rest,' said the lord. 'I shall go out hunting each day, but you shall have breakfast in bed, and get up when you feel like it, and we'll have a game: I will make you a present of whatever I catch in the chase, and you make me a present of whatever you happen to gain during the day.' It is agreed.

Next morning the lord rides out to hunt the deer – and the chase is described. The poet then returns to Gawain having his lie-in and just waking up when, click, he is suddenly wide awake hearing somebody stealthily opening his bedroom door. He peeps through the curtain and sees coming towards him the beautiful wife of the lord of the castle. He feigns to be asleep, she slips through the curtain and sits on his bed, and he pretends to wake with a start. He greets her gallantly: 'Forgive me for sleeping so long. I'll quickly get up and get dressed and join you downstairs.' 'I've a better idea,' she replies: 'everyone's out hunting, and I've locked the door. Let me get into bed with you.' At some length, but with the greatest courtesy, Gawain excuses himself – but allows the lovely lady to give him a kiss before she leaves him. That evening the lord of the castle gives him a haunch of venison, and Gawain gives him one kiss.

The next day follows a similar pattern. The lord hunts the boar, the lady again tries to seduce Gawain – but is resisted, then allowed to give him two kisses. In the evening he is presented with the boar's head, and he gives the lord two kisses.

So to the third day, New Year's Eve. Gawain has not slept well. He knows tomorrow he must play the game and meet that Green Man and his axe. It's his last day. The lord goes hunting the fox, and again the lovely lady comes to Gawain's bedroom, looking more desirable than ever in a smashing dress which sweeps to her ankles but the bodice of which leaves very little to the imagination. And Gawain, on this the last day of his life, still resolutely walks the tightrope between bad faith to his host and discourtesy to a lady. Finally she gives up trying to seduce him, but adds in so many words, 'Darling, won't you give me something to remind me of you.' 'I've only come with little luggage – I've nothing worthy to give you.' 'Well, at least let me give you something,' – and proffers her ring. 'Dear Lady, not having anything to give you, I can't allow you to give anything to me.' 'Well, let me just give you a trifle – my girdle,' and she slips it off her hips. He won't touch it. 'Oh, come on,' she says; 'it's only a belt – though as a matter of fact it's rather a special one. Anyone wearing it can't be killed.' And Gawain wavers ... and then gives way – and she gives

31

him three kisses and leaves him. That evening when the lord comes home, Gawain gives him three kisses and is given the skin of the fox.

New Year's Day. Gawain goes out into the wilds and finds the Green Chapel, 'the most evil holy place I ever entered,' he said – a ruined pile of stones, like an entrance to the underworld. The icy air is loud with one single sound – of an axe being sharpened. The Green Man comes to meet him, compliments him on keeping his faith, tells him to take off his helmet and prepare to be repaid for the blow he dared to strike a year ago. Gawain obeys, bows his head, and the axe is lifted, whirled round, then poised to fall – but is lowered. It is raised a second time, whirled, poised – and lowered again. It is raised the third time, whirled, poised – and comes crashing down – but misses, only nicking the skin of the neck. Gawain leaps aside, draws his sword, and says: 'That's it. You've had your turn, and I've kept my faith. I owe you no more, and now am ready to fight you.'

And the Green Man answers, 'Well said. You've proved yourself. Our Christmas game is over. Your honour and truthfulness have only failed once. You may not recognize me, but I am your host of these last days. We agreed to exchange our winnings each evening. My wife kissed you once, then twice – and you paid me those kisses with complete honour, which is why I didn't bring the axe down the first two times. But you failed in one particular on the third day: you gave me my wife's three kisses; you did not give me her girdle. That was deceitful of you – but your motive was wholly good, which is why I only nicked your neck. Your motive was good: you loved life more than death – and so God's creatures should.'

Gawain admits his fault, leaves the Green Man, returns to Arthur and his court, tells his story concealing nothing, and all are merry and applaud him for having added considerably to the renown and honour of the Round Table.

Well, that's the story, a very prosaic summary of a marvellous work of literature. But what's it got to do with Christmas? If we are puzzled it is perhaps because we've forgotten what Christmas is really about. We so easily allow all the familiar and dearly loved pictures of a crowded inn, crude stable, ox and ass, a lowly couple, rough shepherds, rich kings and a bright star in a sky full of angels – we allow all that to distract our attention from the child in the crib, who he is, and why he's come. Why has he come? When he grew up he answered that question precisely: 'I am come that they might have life and have it more abundantly' (John 10:10).

Christians have too often forgotten that, and appeared more interested in denying life and its joys. But the medieval poem of which I've been speaking says 'Yes' to life: Merriment and joy, laughter and fun and games, are what God wants his children to have. It doesn't pretend there are no difficulties, no miseries, no suffering, no death – but it does say that these should be seen in proper perspective, kept in their place, and not permitted to get us down. So, 'God rest you merry, gentlemen'.

But, but – we live in a bleak midwinter, in a world that is desperately cold and dark. There hangs over us all the threat of something more powerfully deadly than any Green Man's axe. We must assuredly not belittle the threat of a nuclear cataclysm. But let us not kill ourselves with fear.

In the *Church Times* some time ago, Monica Furlong concluded a series of articles on the nuclear arms debate with these words:

> If we don't love life and one another perhaps it matters very little what gets destroyed. In our determined struggle NOT to deny the danger ... there has to be a corresponding lightness of heart, of laughter, of joy, to remind us that life is after all worth living. Nothing will take us more surely down the deadly paths of war than depression and despair.

I believe that is profoundly true. It is the truth that *Sir Gawain and the Green Knight* affirms and celebrates with such verve and humour and joyous confidence – and it has its root in this faith: that the Christ child born in Bethlehem came that we might have life and have it more abundantly. So –

God rest you merry, gentlemen,
Let nothing you dismay,
Remember Christ our Saviour
Was born on Christmas day,
To save us all from Satan's power
When we were gone astray:
O tidings of comfort and joy.

ST JOHN THE EVANGELIST
(27th December)

The Dawn of Truth

A man once saw the dawn with more than ordinary delight. He had lost his way in a dark wooded valley and was overjoyed to see in the growing light that, at the valley's end, the ground sloped steeply upwards out of the trees to the shoulders of a high hill already bright with sunshine. He resolved to tackle the climb – only to find a leopard in the way. A little later a lion appeared, then a wolf. All his good resolutions evaporated and he fled back to the forest he hoped he had escaped.

Thus Dante begins the *Divina Commedia* to tell how, in middle-age, and not unsuccessful by the world's standards, he realized that over the years he'd got bogged down in a spiritual condition he knew to be unworthy. Glimpsing a nobler life he resolved to mend his ways and to climb the sunny hill. But alas for his good resolutions. The leopard, lion and wolf have been variously interpreted – as Lust, Pride and Avarice, for example, or Youth, Manhood and Age. Dante probably derived them from Jeremiah (5:6) and perhaps associated them with St John's verse about 'the lust of the flesh, the lust of the eyes and the pride of life' (1 John 2:16). In the face of these his resolutions came to nothing and he was back where he was before. Indeed, he had to go a very long way down to discover the truth about himself and so get the strength to climb into the sunshine.

Perhaps we experienced something on Christmas morning which made us determine to get out of the muddy rut we secretly know we are in. But that was two days ago, and what's happened since? The chances are we've already been turned back by the beasts. Good intentions don't take us far, and we have yet to learn that the truth about ourselves is worse than we like to think. In the words of St John (whose day this is): 'If we say that we have no sin, we deceive ourselves and the truth is not in us. If we confess our sins, he is faithful and just to forgive us our sins, and to cleanse us from all unrighteousness' (1 John 1:8–9).

HOLY INNOCENTS
(28th December)

The Cornered Rat

THERE is an old custom, or was until recently, that on the night of 28 December, a peal is rung from certain church towers with the bells half-muffled, sending out over the housetops a sound of peculiar poignancy in muted memory and gentle celebration of the deaths of certain children, the Holy Innocents, those boys of Bethlehem of two years old and under whom Herod had killed in an attempt to exterminate the new-born King of the Jews.

Inured as the twentieth century has become to the extreme cruelty of which human beings are still capable, we can still feel horror at the story of that massacre. And the horror is felt all the more keenly because the massacre was the direct result of the birth of Jesus. There comes into the world one who is announced as the world's Saviour and the Prince of Peace – and this leads immediately to the murder of children. It is almost as though the forces of evil, recognizing the extreme menace to their authority which the coming of Jesus portended, intensified to a new pitch of viciousness their determination to destroy the good.

And this could well have been the case. Again and again the appearance of a new good is followed by a manifestation of evil stronger and more malevolent than hitherto experienced. The greater the saint, the greater the temptations. The whitest wall is defaced with the dirtiest graffiti. A newly planted tree that brings the promise of some grace to an ugly environment is uprooted by vandals – but the nearby bed of nettles they spare. Moses seeks to free the children of Israel from slavery, and Pharaoh instantly turns the screw tighter. A possessed boy is brought to Jesus, and the evil spirit within him tears him more savagely than ever. Even ordinary and not very heroic Christians like ourselves have only to make a good resolution, and within twenty-four hours we are more fiercely tempted than we have been for months. We should expect and so be prepared for this. But we should not be discouraged, still less deflected or persuaded that what we are trying to do is beyond the power of God to effect. The cornered rat is the fiercest; he is still cornered.

EPIPHANY

Wise Men's Faith

O F the many stars of which the Bible tells, none is of greater
magnitude than that superstar which now makes its regular
annual appearance in the skies of our minds at the season of
Christmas and which was first observed by wise men of the East
(Matthew 2:1–12). Those astrologers interpreted its rising as signi-
fying the birth of a child to be King of the Jews. And such was
their faith in the meaning of that starry revelation and in the
importance of the prince to which it pointed that they set out on
a long and difficult journey to find him and do him homage.

But, as is its manner, faith didn't take them the whole way nor
answer all their questions. It took them naturally enough to the
land of the Jews, to its capital, to the palace within the capital. But
then there was a check. They were kept waiting. There was apparently no young prince in the palace, and the king seemed to know
less than they themselves. He questioned them closely, and then
told them to go and try in a village not far away and, if they were
successful, to come back and tell him. With that, they were shown
to the door and into the night.

However, none of those things led them to despair or to lose
their faith – for they were wise men. They were not ashamed to
admit the limits of their knowledge or the incompleteness of their
faith – for they were wise men. Even though the information
given them came from the book-knowledge of priests and
lawyers; even though those same professional keepers of ancient
things showed no disposition to go themselves in the direction to
which their knowledge pointed; and even though the information
perhaps seemed unlikely to be relevant, the travellers were ready
to attend to that information and put it to the test – for they were
wise men. And so it came to pass that, when the bright lights of
Herod's palace were behind them and they were out again in the

dark, the original revelation was renewed and 'the star which they saw in the east went before them till it came and stood over where the young child was.'

Even so, Lord, make us wise, confirm our faith, and lead us to thyself.

After the Holydays

THE wise men going home were not the men they had been on their way to Bethlehem. They had made a new beginning. The same may be said of Jesus after his going up to Jerusalem for Passover when he was twelve. Not that much is known of what he experienced on that occasion. The Gospel narrative is reticent. It only states that he stayed behind when his parents started for home; they missed him, returned and searched anxiously – and found him in the Temple. Asked for an explanation he replied (his first recorded words): 'What made you search? Did you not know that I was bound to be in my Father's house?' (Luke 2:49 NEB). They had not realized – perhaps he had not realized it himself until now – that he was no longer the boy he had been. He had become conscious of a special relationship with God, and this meant a great change for him. His priorities were altered, and it was his present overriding obligation to 'be about my Father's business' (AV). The NEB 'in my Father's house' is probably more accurate, but it meant more than just being inside a sacred building as a casual sightseer. It meant, among other things, getting involved in what was happening, listening to the teachers, questioning them, and himself finding answers to the questions they put to him. It was all part of a new beginning for him.

But only the beginning of a new beginning. It did not mean that henceforth *everything* was different, that he had no further obligation to Mary and Joseph and nothing further to learn from them. On the contrary 'he went back with them to Nazareth, and continued to be under their authority'. Another eighteen years' apprenticeship were still to be served.

Those who make new starts may quickly find their priorities altered. But it does not follow that there is nothing more to be learned or that the old routine will be radically changed. In an age which is impatient for quick and sensational results and to be free of all leading strings, this is a hard lesson to learn – and few be they that can swallow it.

LENT

The Still Centre

CONSIDER a revolving wheel – the outer rim linked by spokes to the axle at the hub. The wheel is turned by power coming from the centre and the spokes convey that power to the rim. We know that a mark, say, halfway down a spoke moves round slower than a mark out on the rim – it describes a much smaller circle in precisely the same time. The nearer the mark is to the wheel's centre, the slower it will revolve; and it is, I believe, true to say that at the very centre where the spokes meet and whence the driving force comes, at the very centre of the revolving wheel, there is theoretically a point which is utterly and completely still.

Or – and I take the image from Charles Williams's novel *The Greater Trumps* – consider a busy road junction where four or five important streets meet and the traffic lights have broken down. There is a constant movement of vehicles of all kinds from and to all directions, and a constant roar of engines. Yet there is no confusion because, in the very centre of the circling traffic, there stands a helmeted, white-cuffed figure. He is silent, still, rooted to that central spot; yet he controls all and imposes order upon all. There is nothing stiff or death-like about his stillness; from time to time his arms and hands move deliberately and imperiously, and his body turns decisively within two or three square feet. But in contrast to all the noise and movement that is going on around him, the policeman on point duty is silent and still.

So also – and the idea will be familiar to readers of 'Burnt Norton' – in the midmost point of the whole creation, at the still centre, God is – as he was in the beginning and ever shall be. Around him all is motion, sound, change, decay – galaxies circling, seasons and years and centuries circling, tides ebbing and flowing, sap rising and leaves falling, blood going round and round in the bodies of lions and men and mice. At the still centre, controlling all, moving all, Lord of all power and might, God is. With him there is no variableness, neither shadow of turning; he is the same yesterday, today and for ever.

Less regular and orderly than the movements of heavenly bodies and earthy bloodstreams are the gyrations of sinful men and women, we who in our less giddy moments are conscious of him who is Alpha and Omega, our maker and our judge and in whom we live and move and have our being. One such was Elijah, who was caught up in the whirl of Israelite power-politics in the ninth century BC. One day he stood on Mount Carmel, supreme and alone as the one prophet of God; the day after he was down in the valley and flying for his life from the wrath of Jezebel. His high and exultant faith had melted away, and reaching the desert he laid himself down under a juniper bush and desired to die. In the stillness of the night in the desert new strength came to him, and on he went, on deeper into the desert, until he came to Horeb, the mount of God. And there he found faith and courage again, found them in the Lord. And where did he find the Lord? Not, we are told, in the roaring of the wind, nor in the commotion and convulsion of the earthquake, nor in the terrible power of the fire – but in a still small voice. He had reached the still point at the centre.

Eight centuries later God himself came down from heaven and through taking flesh entered the revolving stream of change and decay and lived in the midst of giddy twisting humans. And one of his most telling characteristics was his stillness. In Jesus, busy and giddy and demented people found peace and repose. 'Come unto me, all that travail and are heavy laden, and I will refresh you,' he invited them. So Mary came and sat at his feet and was still, and busy Martha was urged to do likewise. Lunatics were found sitting at his feet, composed and in their right minds. And the words that he spoke were neither clever chat nor idle gossip, neither vulgar boasting nor loud opinion; such words as he spoke were recognized as words of love, of truth, and of no ordinary power and authority. Experienced boatmen panicked around him, but Jesus had merely to say to the elements, 'Peace, be still,' and there was a great calm. Even when the wildest cyclone of human sin and demonic evil broke upon him, his stillness remained. Cross-examined by men bent upon his destruction, he held his peace — he *held* his peace. Nailed to the cross, he remained unmoved while men made circles round him and taunted him to prove his divinity by coming down from the cross. Being the person he was, he stayed where he was — at the still centre; and, as many of those who have not called themselves Christians have recognized since, he mastered that scene on the green hill and was not mastered by it.

For the still centre is the source of all life and power and might. At the still centre of the cross, immense power was generated, radiating a pardon and peace that we know yet; and from the still centre of the tomb resurrection came. Judas, so dizzy with his twistings that he could not keep still, went and hanged himself. But those others who had been closest to Jesus, after the first panic, came together again and with much fear if not with much faith, with much love if not with much hope, waited, kept still and so witnessed the risen Lord and were filled with his power.

'Be still and know that I am God' (Psalm 46:10): so we are commanded, as the winds and waves of the Sea of Galilee were commanded. We are to be still because, by that means, we may come closest to God, to the core and centre of all things. We are to be still because, by that means, we may sit at his feet, clothed and in our right minds and able to hear the still small voice. We are to be still because, by that means, we may be delivered from dizziness and business and may find both the peace that passes understanding and the source of all power and might. 'Be still and know that I am God.'

But it is important to be clear about what that command means and what it does not mean. In the first place it means that we must be silent — not completely and perpetually of course, though there are some in every generation whom God calls into complete silence. But the majority of us are called to serve and know God in the world and not apart from it; and it is demanded of us that we should be much more silent than we generally are, that we should be quicker to hear and slower to speak. It is instructive that

Christ's command to the storming wind and waves, 'Be still', is literally, in the Greek, 'Be muzzled' or 'Be gagged'. So many have so much to say so loudly today, that we cannot easily hear a still small voice through the pandemonium which masquerades as free speech. In such circumstances it is a high duty for Christians to set an example of patience, restraint and control of their own free speech, to think before they utter and to pray before they think.

In the second place the command, 'Be still', means that we are, as far as our creaturely state allows, to be motionless from time to time; to go into desert places and rest a while; to use periodically such abstinence, that our flesh being subdued to the spirit, we may obey the godly motions that radiate from the still centre; and not only in Lent but at all times the command, 'Be still', means we are to strive to be unbusy, unanxious, unhurried. We are to consider the lilies of the field and not be over-anxious about the morrow. We are to choose with Mary the better part and sit down at the feet of God and not always be cumbered with much serving. Still more are we to be at pains not to become busy little revolutionaries for ever coming and going and plotting and scheming and twisting and turning. Remember Judas Iscariot.

And thirdly, the command, 'Be still', does not mean that we are to be inactive and doing nothing, sleepy as dormice, stagnant as scummy ponds. On the contrary, the stillness of God is a stillness that is vibrant with energy, the stillness that is the source of all power and might and life; as the still point at the axle-centre drives the wheel, as the policeman on point duty controls the traffic. So much human activity is worthless and ineffective today simply because the actors lack authority and power and control; and they lack authority and power and control because they are not still at the centre, but fritter away their energies in ungodly motions doing nothing significant – like the batteries of a car that has been put away with its lamps left on, lamps which blaze away all night illuminating nothing but the inside of the garage doors. Therefore we are commanded not just to be still but, 'Be still, and know that I am God'. Be still, and in the stillness of true prayer (not in the chatter which often passes for prayer) know that God *is* and that he is Lord of all power and might. Then, having come into the centre and been still and known God, we find ourselves full of power and might – and out we must go, for the divine energy won't have it otherwise – out we must go that in our several ways we may bring others back into the stillness to know the greatest of all secrets, to know God. He will not be known in sound and fury, as Elijah discovered; pandemonium is the noise of all devils. But God is known in the still small voice, and to hear that voice and to reach that still centre we have to learn to be very still ourselves.

Getting to Grips

O UR hands are almost the most significant members of our bodies. No doubt our thinking minds and speaking mouths are the features which most obviously distinguish us from all other animals, yet there is reason to believe that neither our minds nor our mouths would now function as they do had not our earliest ancestors taken the momentous step which led to the development of human hands. At an earlier stage certain quadrupeds had taken to living in trees, using their forefeet to help them climb and swing among the branches. But our ancestors, for a variety of reasons and after a time, came down to earth again – came down from the trees when their forefeet had become hands, but hands not yet overspecialized for tree-top life. Like their simian relatives our ancestors had hands that could grip branches and fruit, but hands still capable of all-round development to get a grip on a wide range of other objects as well.

The primary use of our hands is to get a grip on things: knobs and levers and handles and things as various as needles and mud – and the hands of other persons. So Jesus, for instance, is recorded as having grasped a scroll, a whip, the hand of a girl. On one instructive occasion he used his hands to grasp and save a sinking man who, seeing his Master walking over the sea, had himself climbed out of the boat in an ecstasy of faith and started walking over the water. But when he saw the violence of the wind and the waves his faith failed and he began to sink, and Jesus had to reach out his hand and catch hold of him and help him back into the boat (Matthew 14:28–33).

Years later that same Peter was to write: 'Humble yourselves ... under the mighty hand of God' (1 Peter 5:6). Having himself experienced the saving grip of the Lord's hand, he encouraged his readers to let God get a grip on them. And many Christians have for centuries done exactly that at the end of every day, committing themselves to God's safe-keeping for the night with the selfsame words with which Christ committed himself at the hour of his death: 'Father, into thy hands I commend my spirit' (Luke 23:46).

Christ the Maker

Jesus, aware that all had now come to its appointed end, said in fulfilment of Scripture, 'I thirst.' A jar stood there full of sour wine; so they soaked a sponge with the wine, fixed it on a javelin, and held it up to his lips. Having received the wine, he said, 'It is accomplished!' He bowed his head and gave up his spirit. (John 19:28–30)

'He said "It is accomplished" '; in the Authorized Version, 'He cried with a loud voice'. All four gospel writers mention that loud cry just before the end. It is John who records what the cry was: in Greek, '*Tetelestai*'; in the Latin of the Vulgate, '*Consummatum est*', in the English of the Authorized Version, 'It is finished'; in the English of today, 'It is accomplished'. Not 'It's all up', or 'It's the end'; those in defeat do not advertise their surrender at the tops of their voices. But 'It is accomplished' – the triumphant proclamation of an aim realized, a task fulfilled, something of great value achieved – the achievement bringing with it that sense of release and freedom and elation that properly accompanies the completion of something that a man has well and truly made – be it the ploughing of a straight furrow or the completion of a Mass in B Minor, a thing made that is right and lovely, a finished work of art.

In the course of one of his own unfinished poems, 'The Book of Balaam's Ass', David Jones has a passage in which he sets down in a series of disarmingly simple sentences what it is that such a work of art – 'a finished beauty' he calls it – does to us and for us:

... the finished beauty that wins enchantment, gathers worship, holds the minds of men, becomes a word to work powerfully, generates makers' marvels, is a star for us, breaks our contingent misery with the noise of its perfection, day by day wins exaltation for us. (*The Roman Quarry*)

And that may be said not only of the works of a Shakespeare, a Bach or a Picasso, but equally of any master craftsman such as the ploughman, the engraver, the smith and the potter whose concentrated skill and conscientious attention to the finish of their works are celebrated in Ecclesiasticus 38. In a good Anglo-Saxon six-letter word they were all *wrights*, working craftsmen. Alas, the word has become virtually obsolete except in surnames — Cartwright and Wainwright, Wheelwright and Arkwright — though some still speak of shipwrights, and more of playwrights — and we're all still familiar with wrought iron. But it's a thousand years since the word was applied to Jesus — the gloss in the Lindisfarne Gospels translating Mark 6:3 — 'Is not this the wright, the son of Mary?' Which reminds us that he who cried from the cross 'It is accomplished' spent the greater part of his life as a village craftsman — a carpenter, a wright, a joiner as we should call him nowadays — that is, one whose art lay in joining, putting together, different bits of this and that to make something other, something other that would give service and delight to his neighbours.

That is to say, he who was doing something, making something, on the cross, so that there came a moment when he could exclaim, 'It is accomplished' — this person was one whose only apprenticeship had been served in making things and was therefore well versed in *what goes into the making of an artist*. Five things in particular:

First: having a vision of what might be, and using the imagination to see this and that becoming that other which the vision has put before him.

Secondly: exercising a most patient respect for the raw materials, learning all about them, the way they go, what they can do and what they can't do — and bending himself to them almost as much as he bends them to himself.

Thirdly: knowing his tools, loving and valuing them as parts of himself, exchanging this one for that as the work requires, and using them always with an exquisite precision and a most disciplined control.

Fourthly – and this point is often overlooked: recall that for most artists one of the most difficult problems is getting the right things in exactly the right place. I suspect that one of the persistent headaches – or is it heartaches? – of an artist is placing each object, and therefore each stroke of pencil or brush, in such a way that it is neither too big nor too small; neither too weighty nor too light; and that one of the truest ways to bring out the significance of an object is not to score the paper with a heavy line, not to use a more strident colour, but to surround the object in question with a space of no significance. I say 'space of no significance', for that is what it is to the casual observer. But of course it is nothing of the sort. That area of no apparent significance is of incalculable importance to the whole – as are empty spaces, free of clutter, in a church; as are the rests in a musical score; as are the silent spaces in our own lives. We all know the perils of voids, and what the devil can do with the idle. But it is time we remembered how much has been contributed to the growth of man by the existence of the wilderness.

Fifthly: from start to finish, having the faith and the courage to begin, to carry on and to complete the work – whatever the cost in time, in concentration, in weariness, and whatever the cost in strength required to resist the temptation to lose hope and give up in despair, and the temptation to sell the soul and settle for the second-rate or some other form of insincerity. There is not one of us – for man is a maker by nature in a way no other animal is, and there is something of an artist in each one of us – there is not one of us who does not know something of what it costs to make something that is honest and true, lovely and of good report – be it an essay, a letter or a poem, the singing of an anthem or the rowing of a race, the creating of a painting or the baking of a loaf. In each case, *mutatis mutandis*, we undertake something the beginning of which can be really fearful; the carrying on of which is demanding, even exhausting; and the end of which we can only see in imagination. To quote David Jones again:

Making a work is not thinking thoughts but accomplishing an actual journey. There are the same tediums: strugglings with awkward shapes that won't fit into the bag, the same mislayings, as of tickets, the missings of connections, the long waits, the misdirections, the packing of this that you don't need and the forgetting of that which you do, and all such botherations, not to speak of more serious mishaps. (*The Anathemata*, Preface)

These, surely, were at any rate some of the lessons learned amidst the sawdust and shavings of the joiner's shop and artist's studio in Nazareth: the primacy and authority of vision and the need to exercise imagination; immense respect for the raw materials; the loving care and disciplined use of tools; the importance of silent spaces; and the realization that the making of anything worthwhile – that which is true, honest, pure, lovely and of good report – is not thinking thoughts but accomplishing an actual journey which does not end until the work is accomplished and the artist can say: 'It is finished.'

So the Christ's journey started literally enough with a going out to John at a riverside, on through a wilderness, thence round and about in Galilee and Judaea, and finally up, up, up – up to Jerusalem, up to an Upper Room, up to the top of a hill, up onto the cross. Throughout the journey he kept before him the vision of what was to be made and the imagination to see *how* it was to be made. His tools were his hands, his words, his prayers. And his raw materials – very raw in the majority of cases – were the things and the persons encountered on the way. These he treated with infinite patience and respect, making the best of the best in each *and* making the best of the *worst* in each – accepting all their miscellaneous variety, their knottiness, their flaws, their unamenableness, their hardness, with no surrender of his own integrity or faith or hope or love – and making of all this, through his art and craftsmanship and use of silent spaces, nothing less than the salvation of the world and the beginnings of the New Creation.

This was the thing wrought by the son of Mary, the work of art finally accomplished on the cross:

the finished beauty that
wins enchantment,
gathers worship,
holds the minds of men,
becomes a word to work powerfully,
generates makers' marvels,
is a star for us,
breaks our contingent misery with the
   noise of its perfection,
    and day by day wins exaltation for us.

MAUNDY THURSDAY

Bread and Blessing

SIMON Peter was one of the two detailed by Jesus to go and make ready the Passover (Luke 22:8) – to prepare the Upper Room and see to the provision of whatever was needed for their festival supper. Some hours later, and in the same night that he was betrayed, Jesus 'took *bread* and blessed' (Matthew 26:26; Mark 14:22); Luke and Paul have 'gave thanks' (Luke 22:19; 1 Corinthians 11:24).

He had done this on previous occasions – before the feeding of the multitude, for instance. There was nothing original or surprising about it. It was (and is) customary, at the beginning of every Jewish meal, for the head of the household to do exactly that – take bread into his hands and say some such words as 'Blessed art thou, O Lord our God, King of the world, who bringest forth bread from the earth'.

Using language loosely, we might speak of Jesus 'saying grace'. There is, however, an important difference to be noticed. When a grace is said at the beginning of our meals it often takes the form of a prayer asking for the blessing of God upon ourselves and what we are about to receive. But the Jewish practice which Jesus followed (and which the Christian Church has followed at the eucharist ever since), was not to ask for a blessing from God but simply to bless God himself.

It is confusing that the one Anglo-Saxon verb 'bless' has two related but different meanings: to 'consecrate' and to 'praise'. It is the latter that is meant by the Hebrew word generally translated 'bless' in the Bible – though it appears as 'praise' in the Prayer Book version of Psalm 103:1–2: 'Praise the Lord, O my soul: and all that is within me praise his holy name ... and forget not all his benefits.'

When, therefore, at the Last Supper Jesus took bread and

blessed, he did not so much consecrate the bread as *praise God for his gift of it* – and not for bread only but for everything bread represents: all the life-support God gives his children. In other words, he 'gave thanks'. And the Greeks had a word for thanksgiving – eucharist.

GOOD FRIDAY

I Cannot Come Down

'I am doing a great work, so that I cannot come down.'
(Nehemiah 6:3)

Thus Nehemiah calls out from high up on the city wall of
Jerusalem. He is up on the scaffolding supervising the wall's
reconstruction. The wall has been in ruins ever since the
Babylonians sacked Jerusalem 150 years ago. True, the Jews have
been back from their exile for some time, but apart from repairing
their own dwellings and rebuilding the Temple they haven't done
much to make good the damage. They've been content to live
amongst rubble and ruins. And their neighbours, the Samaritans,
have been glad to see Jerusalem so – a shanty town with a temple
in it. They do not wish to see Jerusalem rise again as a great city.
Now, however, things are happening. Nehemiah has arrived, and
under his energetic leadership the inhabitants have been working
like navvies. They've cleared the rubble, erected scaffolding and
gone far towards rebuilding the walls and re-fortifying the city. All
open attempts by the Samaritans to check the work have been
successfully resisted. So now the Samaritans try a trick. They send
envoys to Nehemiah with a message: 'Let's settle our differences
sensibly round a table. Let's have a conference in one of the
villages in the plain of Ono.' It's a reasonable suggestion and
Nehemiah is sure to come. Then they will pop a sack over his
head and whisk him away. Without him to lead them the inhabitants of Jerusalem will be easily defeated.

So the envoys come with the proposal for the conference.
Nehemiah's answer is short and to the point: 'I am doing a great
work, so that I cannot come down.'

Four or five centuries pass and Jerusalem with its city wall
that Nehemiah built recedes into the middle distance. In the

foreground now is a green hill. In the foreground, however, there is still scaffolding, but of a simple kind, erected for a destructive rather than for a constructive purpose: three vertical poles with horizontal cross-pieces. And there are envoys of a hostile power calling up to the figure on the centre scaffold: 'Ha! Thou that destroyest the temple, and buildest it in three days, save thyself, and *come down* from the cross ... He saved others; himself he cannot save. Let the Christ, the King of Israel, now *come down* from the cross, that we may see and believe' (Mark 15:29–31).

Jesus gave no verbal answer. His answer was to remain where he was on his scaffold, which being interpreted is: 'I am doing a great work, so that I cannot come down.'

He could have come down. He had done many mighty works before this and, as he said when he was arrested, he had only to give the word and twelve legions of angels would be at his side. He could have come down easily enough. And as it would have been an unspeakable relief to have had the nails removed from his hands and feet so too, we might think, would it have been enjoyable to watch the change of expression on the faces of his adversaries. But no – it must not be. Had Nehemiah accepted the invitation of the Samaritan envoys and come down from his scaffold, then the fate of Jerusalem would have been sealed. But more than the fate of Jerusalem is at stake now: nothing less than the fate of the world. If Jesus exercises his divine powers to escape from his cross, then he may save himself – but he will save no one else. For the rest of mankind, including ourselves many centuries later, there will be no City of God – no forgiveness of sins, no resurrection of the body, no life everlasting – nothing but endless existence among the rubble and the ruins, nothing but death, hell and destruction. So at all events he had taught his followers to believe; so his followers today believe; so he believed himself. And therefore he replies, in deed if not in word: 'I am doing a great work, so that I cannot come down.'

What is this 'great work' exactly? What was Jesus doing on the cross? At first sight nothing very much. Certainly nothing spectacular. He was not even saying much. For the past two or three years he had been saying a great deal. But on his cross, he is singularly silent: just seven short sentences and no more. The truth of the matter is that the time for talk is over; it is now time for action: I am *doing* a great work.

Yes, but doing what? The stock answers to the question we all know perfectly well: saving the world, redeeming mankind, paying the price of sin. That is true, but phrases like that have long since lost their cutting edge – today they are just smooth, churchy clichés. What then shall we say Jesus was doing? Quite simply and obviously, he was hanging on the cross. Just 'hanging on'. And 'hanging on' means 'holding out', not giving way, not surrendering, but enduring and suffering. And that is precisely what Jesus was doing: hanging on, not surrendering, but enduring evil in its most concentrated form, suffering everything that the spirit of evil could inflict upon him. The devil had been at him for a long while, of course, but in the last twenty-four hours he had turned on the pressure – tempting him to run away in the Garden of Gethsemane, causing one of his chosen followers to betray him, causing the rest to desert him, the Jews to condemn him, Pilate to sentence him, soldiers to mock and beat him, the crowd to howl for his blood. And Jesus endured it all – without protest, without loss of temper, without the slightest sign of impatience or flinching. And then came the moment when he was nailed to the cross and hung up to die slowly while the soldiers diced for his clothes and the onlookers taunted him to show how clever he was and to come down.

But, 'I am doing a great work, so that I cannot come down.' 'I *am doing* a great work' – not 'I have done a great work'. It's not over yet, and therefore 'I cannot come down.' To come down now, to give up and stop hanging on – that would be surrender. It would show he couldn't take it; it would show that the devil was stronger than God, that the devil could force God to his knees; that evil was the master of God and not God the master of evil. So he cannot come down. And indeed there is more to come, a still greater intensity of evil to be suffered. The devil has one more card up his sleeve: to kill him. And if the great work is to be completed, then that too must be suffered. After that – who knows? He believes he will rise again – but there's no bypass round death.

Friday must come before Sunday, night before the dawn, death before the resurrection. 'I am doing a great work, so that I cannot come down.' He doesn't come down, but hangs on to the end. 'It is finished'; 'Father, into thy hands I commend my spirit.' And so, at about three o'clock in the afternoon, while the earth quakes as though hell itself were shuddering, Jesus goes out into the darkness – and the world goes home to tea, its day's sport with the President of the Immortals being done ...

Only later will it become apparent how much has been achieved, that a start has been made with clearing the ruins and the rubble and that on that scaffold of the cross a key section of the wall of the *New* Jerusalem has been built.

What the moral of all this is for you I leave you to work out for yourselves. Suffice it to say that there is still much of the New Jerusalem to be built and that a Christian's place is up on the scaffolding. We have a great work to do and we must not come down. That you will repeatedly be tempted to come down is certain; how to stay up there Jesus will teach you. How he can help you up again if you fall, he will also teach you. So learn of him now; watch him and see how he stays on his scaffold; how, in the face of every evil, he hangs on, and hangs on – and still hangs on. That is the true meaning of suffering.

EASTERTIDE

Who Says I'm Dead?

OSBERT Lancaster, in his *Classical Landscape with Figures*, gives an unforgettable description of Easter in the Greek Orthodox Church. He writes of the stern observance of Lent, and of Holy Week in particular; of the tolling of bells throughout Good Friday and of the dead Christ's bier being carried in procession round every parish that evening; of the emptiness of the cafés and the universal hush on Holy Saturday when in the churches all is dark save for one candle on the altar.

> Towards midnight the space opposite the great west doors of the Metropolis [in Athens], and of every church throughout the land, is gradually filled by an immense crowd in whom the fasting of the previous week and the unaccustomed gloom of the day ... have induced a nervous condition bordering on hysteria ... A few minutes before midnight the Archbishop emerges attended by two deacons ... and mounting the platform begins the reading of the Gospel. By now a deathly hush, or what passes in Greece for a deathly hush, that is to say an absence of sound that compares not unfavourably with the noise of the small mammal-house on a quiet afternoon, has fallen on the vast crowd, which is maintained unbroken until, on the stroke of midnight, the Bishop pronounces the words '*Christos anesté*', 'Christ is risen'. At this the night is rent by a wave of sound in comparison with which all the noises to which one has grown accustomed on other days of the year are as tinkling cymbals. A massed choir and two brass bands burst into powerful, though different, songs of praise; the guard of honour presents arms with a crash unrivalled even in the Wellington Barracks; every bell in the city, ably assisted by air-raid sirens and factory whistles, clangs out the good news, while the

61

cheering crowds greet their Risen Lord with a barrage of rockets, squibs, Roman candles, Chinese crackers, and volley after volley of small-arms fire discharged by such of the devout, a not inconsiderable proportion, as have come to the ceremony armed.

Most Christians who have lived in Western Europe for the last five or six centuries would probably regard such exuberant behaviour on so solemn an occasion as misplaced and unseemly at best, and at worst as superstitious, scandalous or even downright blasphemous. But I believe that among the Western Europeans who would understand this behaviour was the man whom some consider to be the greatest Florentine artist of the great fifteenth century, Piero della Francesca. He was born fifty miles east of Florence in San Sepolcro, and in the 1450s he painted on the wall of the old town hall a remarkable fresco which Vasari held to be his finest work. At the bottom of the picture sprawling on the earth are four soldiers in so deep a stupor of sleep that you can almost hear them snoring. One lolls with his head back, propped up against the side of a flat-topped altar-tomb of marble which fills the lowest third of the picture. And right in the centre of the picture and stepping out of the tomb is a strong, most upright and slightly frightening figure. The right-hand side of his body is naked, and with his bare right arm he holds a tall vertical staff from which flies a white banner emblazoned with a scarlet cross. The weight of his body is on the right leg which is still down in the tomb, but the left leg is drawn up and its foot planted firmly on the lip of the tomb. In a moment the weight of the body will be transferred to it and the other foot brought up beside it, and Christ will come down and stride away through the heaving bodies of these snoring men who will see nothing as, drowned in sleep, they miss the dawn of the world's new age. But Piero shows Christ as almost posing for his picture in this moment before he steps out – the left hand resting on the raised knee and catching up the winding sheet which has slipped from the other side of the body, the white winding sheet which is bright pink in the light of the rising sun. And Christ is looking directly out at the world with great eyes reminiscent of the eyes of those Christs of the Byzantine mosaics, eyes which seem to say 'I am the living one,' eyes which seem to say even more, which challenge those prepared to meet their gaze with the question: 'Who says I'm dead?'

It is a most exceptional picture – and exceptional not least in this, that it is one of the very few works of art created in Western Europe since the thirteenth century in which Christ is advertised as the *risen* Christ, a Christ pulsating with life and radiating power – instead of a dead or dying Christ, a tortured body on a cross or an exhausted and emaciated corpse over the knees of a mother, a picture of heartbreak, death and defeat.

And this has remained more or less true of the Church in Western Europe to this day. It was not so up to the end of the thirteenth century. It is an unmistakably risen and living Christ whose figure stands sovereign over the doorways of the Romanesque and Gothic cathedrals of France. But since then in Western Europe, we have been preoccupied with sin and death, and with what sin and death did to Christ, instead of being preoccupied with Christ, and with what Christ did to sin and death. It's not like that in the Orthodox Church in Eastern Europe, as we saw at the outset. But here in the West there has been – and there still is – more fear than faith in our Christianity and more gloom than joy. No wonder so many turn their back on us and look despairingly elsewhere for life, for meaning in life, and for the living joy that only a living faith can give.

The Church of the West is too preoccupied with sin and death and with what they did to Christ, instead of being preoccupied with Christ and with what he has done to sin and death. Of course, the New Testament has much to say about the cross, and Paul was proud to preach Christ crucified – to drive home the point that the living Lord he served hadn't evaded suffering and hadn't bypassed death. But read Paul's letters as a whole, and the New Testament as a whole, and you can't miss the fact that those books are the work of people who believed in a *living* Lord. They don't worry or argue about *how* Christ has come alive. What they know is that he *is* alive. They themselves suffered and died all right – and some of them as horribly as their Lord had done. But that

63

didn't make any difference. Paul was certain that *nothing*, not even death, could separate him from the love of God which is in Christ Jesus. And if we were to say to Paul, 'If you knew what we know, you wouldn't be so credulous and superstitious,' he would, I think, reply: 'Believe me, I know credulity and superstition when I see it. People once took me for a god, and I only just managed to stop them from worshipping me. I know superstition when I see it – and I see it in *you*. I see your faith, your credulous super-stitious faith in what you call science but which is for most of you your twentieth-century magic, and I see how frozen you are with fascination and fear of death, so terrified that you can hardly bear to hear the word "cancer" pronounced.'

The fact is that the first Christians simply didn't worry about death. The problem of *how* resurrection works was not much easier for them than it is for us, and certainly they recognized that they must go through the natural process of dying. But they knew that despite the difficulties and contrary to all outward appearances (which were just as obvious to them as they are to us) they had been delivered from death's power. They knew this because they knew themselves to be possessed, driven, vitalized by the *living* Spirit of the *living* Christ:

the living Christ whom the Eastern Church has never forgotten;
the living Christ whom the Western Church worshipped for thirteen centuries;
the living Christ whom Piero della Francesca portrayed on a wall in a town hall in a corner of Tuscany in the fifteenth century;
that Christ whose voice was heard by St John on an island in the Aegean, a voice like a trumpet, saying: 'Fear not, I am ... the living one; and I was dead, and behold, I am alive for evermore, and I have the key of death and the key of hell!'
that Christ who challenges us with the question: 'Who says I'm dead?'

God grant us to hear those words again, to have the courage and humility to accept them as the truth, and to live at all times in the joy that comes from accepting them.

Spring

IT is no mere coincidence that we celebrate the resurrection of Christ at this time of year. He was crucified at Passover time, and the date of Easter is consequently determined by the date of that Jewish festival which, before it became the celebration of the deliverance of Israel from Egypt, was a spring festival of the Hebrew nomads. It was the lambing season; after winter's inclemency, pastures were green again, and 'there was much grass in the place' (John 6:10). For those in the northern hemisphere, therefore, Christ's up-rising is essentially linked with that explosive resurgence of fresh life when sap rises, seeds sprout, buds burst, eggs hatch, bats and other sleepers awake and tadpoles wriggle in ditches. Because of this new beginning of vitality, this explosive leap of life, we call it 'Spring'.

The same word spells another kind of beginning and up-leap and source of vitality – the place where clear clean water bursts out and wells up, the source and fount of brook or stream, of beck or burn or nant, which run together to become the rivers so essential to all that live on the dry land. From earliest times people have venerated springs, and been enchanted by the sight of water bubbling up from subterranean caverns measureless to man – the sand motes dancing, the cresses waving, and the bright water running away over the stones to do its vital work of quenching thirst and refreshing and renewing plant and beast and man. To have a reminder of this spring-head of life, Romans would set a pool in the courtyard of their houses and monks sink a well in their cloister garth – and perhaps there is a distant reminiscence of it in the bird-bath in a twentieth-century garden. And the heart of a great city is subtly and certainly enhanced if there are fountains playing in its squares.

A Christian's devotion may be much refreshed by letting the mind linger on such a sentence as: 'he sendeth the springs into the rivers which run among the hills' (Psalm 104:10). From such a spring welled a stream of thanksgiving which led St Francis to exclaim: 'Praised be our Lord for our Sister Water, which is so very serviceable and humble and clean.'

The Lord of the Dance

JOY tickles the toes as well as the tongue. Always and everywhere men and women express it not only with singing but also with *dancing*. When a sovereign is crowned or a contest won, when good news comes or they fall in love, people don't willingly sit twiddling their thumbs or peeling potatoes. They sing and they dance. Age or infirmity or work-to-be-done may forbid the feet – but cannot forbid the heart to dance when human beings feel they're in step with the rhythms of the universe, with the music of the stars and with the dance of the atoms; when, if they be God-fearing, they sense they are almost in step with God himself and with the pattern of purposes that he has ordained.

Don't be shocked by the suggestion that religion and dancing should go together. The Dance is the mother of most of the rites with which people try to worship God. The Israelites, Puritans as they were in some respects, were not ashamed to praise God's name in the dance. They danced on the beach of the Red Sea after their escape from Egypt. There was dancing when David had killed Goliath, dancing when the Ark was brought back to Jerusalem – and dancing, too, as well as music and fatted calf on that memorable occasion when a prodigal son came home; the only person who disapproved was that singularly unattractive character, the prodigal's elder brother.

In Christian times, too, people have praised God's name in the dance. There's not been much of it in Britain for the last three centuries. The British have been too ready to empty the Christian faith of its gaiety and joy, to narrow religion and make it no more than the grim groove of moral duty. But it was not so in the days of the apostles, and it was not so in the Middle Ages when it was not unusual to think of the Christian life as a Dance and of Christ himself as the Lord of that Dance. The carols people sang they also danced, and one of those carols represents the earthly life of Christ as a dance – that is, a pattern of ordered, graceful steps, a disciplined obedience to certain vital rhythms, a self-forgetting abandon to a pattern of movement ordained by his heavenly

Father. It was at Bethlehem that Jesus joined in with mankind – to bring them out of their sinful confusion, back into step with God, back into the general Dance of the stars and the atoms and the angels. Sometimes the steps Christ footed as he went in and out among us were quick and gay, sometimes they were slow and solemn. But quick or slow, from start to finish his life on earth followed a pattern of graceful, courteous, rhythmic movement in concert with God and with such of us as would be his partners.

But was it not only a Danse Macabre, a Dance of Death, ending – as so many of the sacred dances of primitive peoples ended – in a bloody and useless sacrifice? Most certainly the slow movement of Christ's Dance, the Pavane of his Passion, is not to be forgotten. When Christ came to dance with us he never sat out; he evaded nothing; he permitted Judas to kiss him, and he danced – as all of us must – with death. *But the Dance went on*: the Pavane of the Passion was not the end. For Christians believe, we honestly believe, that on the third day the tempo quickened, the step grew brisker, death had to let go – and Jesus was dancingly alive again and for ever.

Sydney Carter's modern hymn, *The Lord of the Dance*, is based on the medieval carol to which I referred just now:

I danced in the morning when the world was begun,
And I danced in the moon and the stars and the sun,
And I came down from heaven and I danced on the earth;
At Bethlehem I had my birth …

I danced on a Friday when the sky turned black,
It's hard to dance with the devil on your back.
They buried my body and they thought I'd gone;
But I am the Dance, and I still go on.

They cut me down and I leap up high;
I am the life that'll never, never die;
I'll live in you, if you'll live in me:
I am the Lord of the Dance, said he.

Christ does not dance alone. Others were involved. Only the exhibitionist wants to dance alone. Christ asked people to dance with him: 'Follow me,' he said, and took great pains to teach them the steps. Some were too self-conscious or disapproving ever to take the floor. Some soon found the Dance he led them too demanding – and went and sat out. But others joined in with a kind of clod-hopping vigour. In their fishermen's boots they stumbled badly from time to time to begin with. But because they persevered grace gradually came – and their joy was unbounded when the partner they thought they had lost came back and held out his hands to them again. And few who read the Acts of the Apostles can escape the conclusion that they were the acts of men whose hearts were dancing whatever their bodies suffered as they went to the ends of the earth to bring others into the Dance. In the course of time those apostles also came to the Pavane and they too danced with death – but *because* they were still the partners of the dancing Christ they too came to their resurrection and to heaven. This, perhaps, is heaven: perfect life and perfect love, music and dancing, rhythm and melody, grace and courtesy, stars and atoms and beasts and flowers and men and angels – all with Christ, and Christ with God.

Now this is a way of looking at things which can have important, healthy and most liberating consequences for ourselves. For once we have committed ourselves to the belief that our lives are part of an ongoing movement of the whole creation, and that movement a Dance, then a great many things that bewilder us or dismay us will do so no longer. Once we accept that, in that Dance, there is no going back and no standing still, and that only those who are dead in heart or head can drop out – then we realize that it is senseless to make ourselves miserable grieving over the past and wishing the dance had stopped five or fifty miles back, five or fifty years ago. So we abandon ourselves to Christ's Dance in the spirit of which de Caussade wrote when he spoke of the Christian having a duty to abandon himself to the Divine Providence. And we are not to worry now about where the Lord of the Dance will lead us tomorrow – sufficient unto the day is the evil thereof. Dance one day at a time.

Dance one day at a time then – out from God's house on Sunday, through the week's work in the world and back again next Sunday, and following the while the steps which Jesus has taught us and bringing others into the dance. Such a pattern of living is no grim groove of duty but a joyous dance if we've really appreciated what the resurrection means — that Christ danced *through* death. So to follow him demands some energy of heart, intelligence of mind, and suppleness of imagination; an ear for God's music and a sense of his rhythms; a fine sensitivity to what's going on and to the whereabouts of your partners' feet — so that you don't tread on any toes. It demands no little grace, which only Christ can give you, and the faith and patience to keep your balance in the slow and difficult movements. If we are solo exhibitionists, or acutely self-conscious, or lacking the confidence to abandon ourselves to where the Dance leads; and if we are sour, or superior, or censorious — then we shall probably prefer not to join in — and we shall have the prodigal son's elder brother for company outside. But, in the words of the Psalmist, 'Let the children of Sion be joyful in their King. Let them praise his name in the dance' (Psalm 149:2–3).

Pilgrimage

On the Move Again

IT is in all ways, at least in the northern hemisphere, the resurrection season. As the nineteenth-century hymn writer, J. M. Neale, put it:

> The world itself keeps Easter Day ...
> The Lord has risen, as all things tell:
> Good Christians, see ye rise as well!

After the torpor of winter, fresh energy is released by the coming of warmer weather and lengthening hours of daylight. So buds burst and birds sing and bees are busy again. And in various ways human beings too are conscious of a new vitality in themselves. After all those winter evenings spent sitting by the fireside – or whatever has taken its place as the focal point of our homes – we feel stimulated to tackle the garden again or to set about other energetic undertakings out in the open about which we could do no more than dream during winter's shut-down. We share with both plants and animals the urge to get moving again.

And that may well include an urge to get moving a very long way; not just into the garden or down the streets and lanes of the next-door parish, but out beyond the frontier of whatever is our 'homeland'. It is no accident that in one of the greatest and liveliest poems ever written in England, *The Canterbury Tales*, Chaucer brings together in its opening lines springtime in England and the assembly in a south London inn of a group of men and women about to get moving and go on a pilgrimage.

To go on a pilgrimage is one of the oldest activities of man, and the experience can be rich in spiritual significance, whether the pilgrim be a first-century Galilean going up to Jerusalem for the Passover, a medieval European making for Compostela or a twentieth-century student hitching to Delphi or Katmandu. Some of the Psalms were specially composed as pilgrim songs, and St

Peter thought of his readers – and encouraged them to think of themselves – as 'strangers and pilgrims' (1 Peter 2:11). And since this is the resurrection season, it is timely to take pilgrimage as our theme and to explore again the old idea of our life as a pilgrimage.

The Pilgrim's Way

A T the root of the word 'pilgrim' is the idea of one who goes beyond the bounds of his homeland and journeys under foreign skies through a countryside that is strange. A pilgrim is continuously on the move, making his way stage by stage from one unknown place to another – and so long as the pilgrimage lasts he has no base, no home, no familiar place to which he can return for security at the end of the day. Like Abraham, Isaac and Jacob (Hebrews 11:8–16) he has 'no continuing city' (Hebrews 13:14); he does not know where he will get to by sundown; he can only be sure that it won't be where he is now, and that tomorrow evening he will be somewhere else again. And being thus continuously on the move, he has to overcome his instinctive longing for security and certainty with the faith that somewhere ahead lies the place where he will find something that will more than compensate for all the weariness, uncertainty, discomfort and possible danger of the journey.

Moreover, once he has left his own homeland, he will always be among people whose ways and words will be strange to him and in whose eyes he himself will be a foreigner – perhaps an object of suspicion. Differences of custom, law and, above all, language will add greatly to his sense of insecurity – but great will be his joy when he is treated by those through whose land he travels with warmth, hospitality and understanding.

In so far as we think of ourselves, as the New Testament encourages us to do, as pilgrims journeying towards the City of God through a world where we have no continuing city, and continuously exposed to all the uncertainties that such a way of living involves, we shall not be surprised if we meet with much that we do not understand – and we shall experience a particular joy when we are treated by those we encounter with a courtesy and friendliness we have no right to expect. By the same token, we should reflect that those whom we meet as we go about our daily tasks are themselves strangers and pilgrims – reflect, too, on the joy that is ours to give or withhold by the way in which we treat them.

Getting Ready to Go

A pilgrim must make ready. 'He that be a pilgrim,' said a London preacher in 1406, 'oweth first to pay his debts, afterwards to set his house in governance, and afterwards to array himself and take leave of his neighbours, and so go forth' (quoted by Jonathan Sumption, whose book *Pilgrimage: An Image of Mediaeval Religion* is a good antidote to any falsely romantic ideas about the subject). The pilgrim must set his affairs in order before he sets out; he must clear his desk; he must see to it that all who are dependent upon him are properly provided for so long as he is away.

Furthermore, because he is going to be continuously on the move he will be obliged to travel light. Having assembled all he would like to take with him he must then decide, not without pain, what is essential; the rest he must leave behind. Essentials will be a water-bottle; a satchel for his daily bread and his money; a strong all-weather suit of clothes; and a good pair of boots. The old world pilgrim needed a staff, but a guidebook and a phrase book will be more useful to the twentieth-century pilgrim – who may also need a passport, for gone are the days when it was sufficient for him to have a cross embroidered on his tunic.

The person who makes up his mind that, in view of his age, the time has come to him to make a new and more serious start and to set out once more for the City of God should realize that his chances of reaching his objective will be greatly increased if he does some preparation, 'sets his house in governance', checks his equipment and nerves himself to abandon all that is not essential. And he might find it helpful to get into his head the lines Walter Ralegh wrote (probably on the eve of his execution):

> Give me my scallop-shell of quiet,
> My staff of faith to walk upon,
> My scrip of joy, immortal diet,
> My bottle of salvation,
> My gown of glory, hope's true gage,
> And thus I'll take my pilgrimage.

Beginner's Joy

AFTER weeks of anticipation and all the rush and bustle of the last days of final preparation the pilgrim begins his journey with joy. There may be some sadness in taking leave of faces and places which he will not see again for some time – if ever; and there may be some trepidation at the prospect of all the uncertainties that lie ahead of him and at abandoning for the time being all the security and comfort that home spells. But such regrets and fears are quickly displaced once the journey has started.

Not a little of his joy comes from the sensation of 'getting away from it all'. The monotony of his humdrum daily existence – that's gone. The insoluble problems which he has had to live with for so long – they too have disappeared; he has done what he can to resolve them before setting out, and they are now out of his hands and he can do nothing about them for the time being. Instead, his attention is fully occupied by a series of wholly new experiences, sights and sounds never met before, and all the consequences of changing his limited and comparatively sedentary life for a life of continuous movement. He has broken away from the parish pump and all the world is before him. And above all there is the joy that comes of having made a considered decision and hopefully taken the first steps towards its implementation – the attaining of a great objective.

Most of us have known Beginner's Joy at various times – when we were confirmed, perhaps, and on other occasions when we resolved to make a new start. But it is a joy which we can experience every single morning. In a very real sense no day dawns without our being given the opportunity to start afresh, and every day we can make a mini-pilgrimage with the object of being somewhere closer to God by nightfall. Yesterday is gone; today is new. Stationary and humdrum our lives may seem to be, but it remains indisputable that with every dawn we enter upon something of pristine freshness, something that never was before. Granted, hope is a poor supper; but don't forget Bacon also said it makes a good breakfast.

Which is the Way?

ONE of the difficulties we have to face as pilgrims is the problem of finding the way. Just because we are on unknown ground it is inevitable that we shall sometimes be at a loss which road to take; and for the same reason our fellow-pilgrims will not be able to help us.

The difficulty should not be exaggerated. Often enough the way is perfectly plain. There are signposts, and the feet of the thousands who have made the pilgrimage before us have left us a well-worn path. Such a way is part of our inheritance from the past, and is to be accepted and used with humble gratitude. We should be slow to take a short cut however confidently proposed by any wiseacre in the company unless he has made the pilgrimage before; there will be a river down in the valley, and we certainly cannot count on there being a bridge if his cross-country suggestion is followed.

But the fact that thousands have gone before us does not mean that the way is always obvious. And it is in populous places rather than in uninhabited wastes that it is most easily lost. Where there are most people, and they busy with their own affairs, there are too many footprints going in too many different directions. If in doubt it is only sensible to stop at once and ask the way. But that is something many of us are loath to do. It means becoming beholden to someone else; it appears to be a reflection on our competence, an admission of failure; and anyhow we are afraid to betray our limited knowledge of the local language and so look sillier than we like to think we are. To ask for help requires quite a lot of self-sacrifice of a certain kind – and it is a sacrifice men seem to be less willing to make than women.

The pilgrim *en route* for the heavenly City should always be ready to confess his ignorance and not be too proud to ask for guidance when he doesn't know which way to turn. And in such circumstances, and remembering that Jesus called himself 'the way' (John 14:6) it is not so puerile as some might suppose to put to oneself the question: 'What would Jesus do?'

Monotonous Stretches

IN the cloister of the Spanish monastery of Santo Domingo de Silos there is an unusual Romanesque sculpture of Christ with the two disciples on the road to Emmaus – Christ not immediately recognizable since he appears in the guise of a pilgrim, with a pilgrim's hat, staff and wallet, the latter bearing the pilgrim's badge of a scallop shell.

A pilgrimage is not an unbroken string of unending excitements and delightful experiences. The novelty of it all will carry a pilgrim through such difficulties as he may meet in the early stages, but there are many more stages to come and for much of the way the road may well be depressingly monotonous. The medieval pilgrim from, say, Burgundy to Santiago de Compostela had much to enjoy and with which to occupy his mind as he made his way through France and over the Pyrenees. But then he still had five hundred miles to go across Spain, many of them along a way which ran dead straight for miles on end across flat and featureless plains, so that the pilgrimage could well begin to seem even more tedious and much more exhausting than daily life back home.

Monotony, with its dispiriting effects, is as much a part of pilgrim experience as excitement and variety, and it brings its own temptations: to question the value of the pilgrimage, and whether the price to be paid to reach the objective is not beyond the pilgrim's powers. He goes more slowly; he may decide to give up. Most of those who have set out as pilgrims along the Way of Prayer experience such tedious stretches and know such temptations.

Now is the time, as much as in moments of mishap, when the pilgrim is glad of companions to beguile the hours with their tales and encourage his flagging spirits. Now too is the time to recall Luke 24:13–35 which tells how two dispirited wayfarers were joined by a third whose conversation stimulated them to such a degree that they came to the end of that day's journey greatly encouraged, and begged him to stay and have supper with them that they might enjoy his exhilarating company for longer. And in the breaking of bread they recognized their fellow-traveller.

The Difficult Hills

MANY places of pilgrimage lie in hill country, and those who would reach them are therefore required to make extra efforts in the later stages of their journey. The road to Santiago de Compostela, after running monotonously straight across the plateaux of Castile, snakes up into the mountains of Galicia. Jesus going up from Galilee to Jerusalem by way of the Jordan Valley had to climb three thousand feet in the last twenty-five miles.

The extra effort is needed just when the pilgrim's resources have become largely exhausted. The freshness of the early stages has long worn off, the dreary trudge across the levels has produced its own form of fatigue, and stronger every morning is the temptation to delay the start of another day's plod. And what is now called for is not only a greater physical effort: the pilgrim's spirit has got to come to terms with the fact that in hill country the way curls and bends and no longer has that routine directness which may have seemed boring at the time but had the advantage of allowing him to feel that he was travelling as straight as the crow flies. But in the hills crows can't be followed, and the shortest way there is now the longest way round – which is maddening to those impatient to reach the end.

There are compensations, however, and pilgrims along the Way of Prayer should make the most of them instead of letting themselves become discouraged because the going is harder and their rate of progress slower. The wind is colder in the mountains, but more invigorating. New flowers appear at the roadside, and the greater the altitude the more intense their colour. There is the sound of running streams in the silence peculiar to uninhabited high places. And when we pause for breath and look back we can take comfort from seeing how much progress has been made; the top of the pass may still seem far off, but we have only to look back to realize how much nearer it really is.

But while such encouragements should be recognized and appreciated they must not be allowed to delay us unduly. Wild flowers and waterfalls are not what we've come to see, and so long as we are looking back we are getting no nearer our goal.

Was It Worth It?

WITH his objective now clearly visible, and with mounting excitement and expectation, the pilgrim covers the last miles of his long journey. Finally comes the great moment when, having crossed the last river and climbed the last steps, he passes from the outside world through the portals of the building which towers around him, and finds himself within the sacred space of which he has heard so much and with which his mind has been preoccupied for so long.

And what are his reactions? There is grateful relief that he has been brought in safety to his journey's end. But above all he is overwhelmed with awe and wonder at the beauty of the new world into which he has stepped – the beauty, it may be, of august simplicity and stillness or the exciting beauty of glorious richness – and behind all the beauty there is the indefinable atmosphere of a holy and powerful Presence. And, if he is wise, the pilgrim will give himself the opportunity to allow it all to speak to him and refresh him. He will sink down and sit in silence for several minutes before starting to traipse along aisles, down into crypts and up into sanctuaries, staring at relics and goggling at monuments.

But perhaps it isn't like that at all. The pilgrim may be shocked and disappointed to find the whole place thronged with a crowd of others, the silence destroyed by the hubbub of their voices and the clink of coin as they seek to acquire some souvenir as a sign that their pilgrimage has been performed. He wonders if his journey has been worth it, and feels impatient with the crowd and angry with the temple attendants for allowing such apparent desecration.

Such a reaction should be severely suppressed. Maybe the shrine is not being reverenced as we think it should, but we shall best help to mend matters if, instead of breathing flames of irritation and darting flashes of disapproval, we treat our fellows with extra courtesy and make time to pray for them as well as for ourselves. For we have it on the highest authority that it is the pure in heart who will be granted the vision of God which is the end of every pilgrimage (Matthew 5:8).

Back to Square One?

WHEN the pilgrim's journey is done, his destination reached, his devotions paid, he must then set about something on which accounts of pilgrimages are generally silent: he must retrace his steps, steeling himself to face again all the discomforts, difficulties and dangers of the road, and treading once more all those many weary miles in order to get back to where he started.

To begin with this may seem a tedious matter and a sharp anticlimax. After weeks experiencing the freedom and ever-changing scene which wayfarers enjoy, and the mounting excitement which the outward journey gave him, the pilgrim may be depressed by the prospect of a dreary return to the routine of work and domestic duty back home. But there will be compensations; he will be an experienced traveller by now; and most pilgrims on the return journey come to look forward to the moment of homecoming with as much excitement as they looked forward to reaching whatever holy place was the object of their outward journey.

But in fact it is never a case of returning to square one. The home to which the pilgrim returns is never quite the same as the home from which he set out. It will have undergone various changes in his absence – changes ranging from the coming and going of flowers in the garden to births and deaths in the local community. And the greatest change of all will be the change in the pilgrim himself who, in proportion to the variety and intensity of his experiences on his pilgrimage, will be a different person. He will now see his home, his neighbours and his work through new eyes – eyes that have been given all manner of visions and insights on his pilgrimage – and so will bring to his home, his neighbours and his work a new spirit and fresh power.

And perhaps the greatest change of all in him will be that, having once been a pilgrim, he will have learned to be always a pilgrim – one who sees the whole of the rest of his life as a journey (and every day as a stage on that journey) towards the point where he finally crosses the last river to reach the place where trumpets are sounding on the other side.

ROGATIONTIDE

Prayer in Progress

A T this season in earlier years it was common practice for parson and people to go in procession about their parish, beating its bounds and asking for the blessing of God upon the crops and cattle on which the life of the community so much depended. They made a progress and prayed as they went.

Human beings are travellers by nature. But we can – and do – go thousands of miles without putting a foot to the ground and even though we may be bed-ridden. We have only to close our eyes to what is immediately around us and, using our knowledge and our powers of memory and imagination, we can journey to the uttermost parts of the earth – and beyond. And prayer can be a form of such travel, and is experienced at its simplest in intercession when we make a progress about the places where we live; when, going farther afield, we walk up and down corridors of power, hospital wards, marketplaces, or the backstreets of Saigon. As we thus put ourselves alongside our fellows we try, with the Spirit's holy inspiration, to speak with God about their needs.

But will anything come of it? It is perhaps trite to recall Tennyson's assertion: 'More things are wrought by prayer than this world dreams of.' But because something is trite it doesn't follow that it is worthless, and very many have had experiences which – to put it at the lowest – makes it unwise for anyone to be dogmatic and deny the effectiveness of such prayer. What can be said with certainty is that Jesus told his followers to ask God for things.

It should also be added that still more would be wrought by prayer if, having taken Jesus at his word and made our intercession, and having the use of our feet and hands, we go out and find some way of helping God with his answer to our asking. We are to be doers of the word, and not hearers only (James 1:22), and therefore we must pray: *Grant to us thy humble servants, that by thy holy inspiration we may think those things that be good, and by thy merciful guiding may perform the same.*

ASCENSION DAY

Coming Up

THIS week Christians have come to the climax of their annual celebration of that stupendous process which, beginning at Easter with Christ's rising up out of the tomb, culminated in his ascension into heaven – a process symbolized, in the spring of the year, by the rising and climbing up out of the earth and into the sunshine of dormant plants and buried seeds (cf. John 12:24).

Especially significant for animals and man is the coming up of one particular family of plants so widespread, so lowly, so unspectacular in their flowering, that we rarely stop to appreciate their importance – the grasses. But six thousand years ago human beings began deliberately to cultivate certain of those grasses, having discovered that their seeds, ground and baked, made a superb food – bread. Some of that seed they carefully kept for sowing the following year when, given the right conditions and care (and, they thought, the right prayers and sacrifices), each single grain would produce thirty, sixty or even a hundred others (Mark 4:8), and so provide them with their staple food until the following spring when once again they would hope to see repeated the same miraculous process: 'the earth bringeth forth fruit of herself; first the blade, then the ear, after that the full corn in the ear' (Mark 4:28).

So amazing was this annual resurrection and ascension, and the harvest to which it led, that it is understandable that many of our ancestors felt that the earth herself must be divine, a mother-goddess (the Romans called her Ceres, hence our cereals). But, although the children of Israel were often tempted to think along the same lines, they remained fundamentally and finally loyal to their belief that there is only one God, and that it is he alone 'who bringeth forth grass for the cattle and green herb for the service of men; that he may bring food out of the earth ... and bread to strengthen man's heart (Psalm 104:14–15).

A Christian at the eucharist, holding in his hands a small piece of consecrated bread, should sometimes reflect that, in addition to everything else it is and represents, it is the gift of God, the product of his mysterious and marvellous process carelessly called 'natural growth'.

WHITSUNDAY

Prepare – and be Found

There's no positive way. It's rather a negative business – becoming still enough inside to be receptive to it. You can't seek for it, but if you prepare for it it will come and settle on you like an Emperor moth. In fact, not 'seek and ye shall find' as the Bible says, but 'prepare and ye shall be found'.

The quotation comes from Lawrence Durrell's novel *The Dark Labyrinth*, and the words were spoken by an old lady, an American called Ruth Adams, in a lost world high up in the mountains of Crete. How she had got there does not concern us now, although that story is not without significance for those who feel themselves to be lost in the dark, their lives trapped in a labyrinth of insoluble complexity. Suffice it to say that twenty-one years earlier Ruth Adams and three companions had been exploring some caves when the roof behind them had collapsed. They were trapped and lost in the dark, but miraculously or accidentally (depending on your point of view) they had stumbled on a way out of the dark maze of caves and found themselves in a kind of garden of Eden high up in the mountains – only to discover that there was no way out save by the way they had come. They were cut off from the world by unscalable precipices. Two of Ruth's companions had gone back by the way they had come, and that was the last anyone had seen of them. They had presumably perished in the labyrinth. Her other companion had been her brother Godfrey, a man of much ingenuity who had set himself to devise ways and means of keeping himself and his sister alive.

But [said the old lady] somehow he began to get upset when year succeeded year and there seemed less and less to do. He was a victim of activity. At first he used to call this place a heaven; but he was the kind of man who would get discontented with heaven itself. He was in love with mountains – and well known as a climber in his day. To be marooned here and surrounded by unclimbable mountains was too much for him. He tried to climb out, back into the world, but lost his foothold. He fell a clear seven hundred feet.

But the old lady had settled down to her total isolation – or rather, she had suddenly realized that although she was completely isolated she was not alone. And this realization came, she said, through repose:

'How can I put it? On a dark night you try to find the keyhole in the front door. You cannot. That is what our lives are normally like. Then at last your key suddenly slides into the groove and you are master of your house again. A half-second of relief and power. And another thing. This experience I felt was not an extraordinary one. It came out of ordinary faculties, through repose. I had never been still enough before. Here I got as still as a needle ... Are you listening? ...

'I remembered how life was before,' pursued the old lady quietly. 'I was outside everything in a certain way. Now I participate *with* everything. I feel joined to everything in a new kind of way. Before I lived by moral precepts – for morality is an attempt to unite ourselves to people. Now I don't feel the need for religion, or faith in the old sense. In my own mind inside ... I no longer prohibit and select. I include. It's the *purely scientific* meaning of the word "love". Does it sound rubbish? Do you understand a word I say?'

... 'How do you ... did you ... find it? I mean the feeling?'

For a long time the woman said nothing, she arched her brows as if she were trying to locate within herself the sources of the spring. At last she said: 'I don't know.' She closed her eyes. 'There's no positive way. It's rather a negative business – becoming still enough inside to be receptive to it. You can't seek for it, but if you prepare for it, it will come and settle on you like an Emperor moth. In fact, not "seek and ye shall find" as the Bible says, but "prepare and ye shall be found".'

It was Jesus who said: 'Seek and ye shall find.' The saying is recorded by both Matthew and Luke, and in Luke's Gospel the saying is specifically linked with seeking and finding the Holy Spirit. 'If ye ... know how to give good gifts unto your children,' said Jesus, 'how much more shall your heavenly Father give the Holy Spirit to them that ask him?' But we may be allowed to question whether St Luke rightly reported Jesus here. It wholly *contradicts* what Jesus says elsewhere of the Holy Spirit. He's like the wind, Jesus said. The wind blows as and where and when it likes. It's quite unpredictable. We humans cannot control it. And the Holy Spirit is like that. He cannot be controlled by us. His coming cannot be compelled.

That the coming of the Holy Spirit cannot be compelled as and when we mortals decide was certainly true of his coming the first Whitsunday. The apostles did not find him by seeking him. They were *found by* him as they were gathered together in an upper room. He settled on them as they waited — had been waiting ten days. They were still, passive, negative — simply waiting. Jesus had told them to be so. It was the last thing he told them before he left them. Wait. Sit still and wait. 'Tarry ye in the city, until ye be clothed with power from on high.' Don't go searching; don't go rushing about here and there looking for the Spirit that shall guide you and give you power. Wait. Wait. Be still.

It's a lesson most Christians need to learn again. That the Church today sorely needs a new outpouring of the Holy Spirit is obvious enough. We need his power, his light, his guidance, his strength. We need him above all to unify us, to teach us again what love really is — that we may be joined together, to each other and to everything else, in a new kind of way.

But the coming of the Holy Spirit is not to be compelled. We can pray for him to come — indeed, we've been specifically told to do so. But there's no active and positive way of making him come as and when and where we wish. Rather is it a negative business of being prepared – of becoming still enough inside to become receptive to him. And this is very difficult at the present time. The Church as a whole, Christians in general, are fast becoming, like the rest of the Western world and like the old lady's brother, victims of activity. We must, we feel, be up and doing, arranging meetings, attending meetings, writing up meetings, setting up commissions, drawing up reports, devising new liturgies, new administrative machinery, marching, demonstrating, protesting – *doing* something. But that sort of impatience only leads to increased frustration and dissatisfaction and can end in disaster – in losing one's foothold in a fall of seven hundred clear feet.

If we really want the power and the guidance of the Holy Spirit that is not the way to go about it – whatever our activist friends may say. Of course there must be action in the end, Christian action – but it won't be *Christian* action unless it is first directed and empowered by God the Holy Spirit. And God the Holy Spirit will only come to those who are still enough to be receptive to him.

You can't seek for him, but if you prepare for him he will come and settle on you – as he came and settled, like a dove, on Jesus himself at his baptism, as he came and settled on the apostles on the first Whitsunday. In fact – not 'seek and ye shall find', but 'prepare and ye shall be found'. And *then* we shall be united – joined to each other, and to everyone and everything else – in a new kind of way: the fellowship of the Holy Spirit.

A Windy Day

THE outgoing movement of the apostle-witnesses of Jesus was powered by the Holy Spirit which hit them with something like hurricane force when the day of Pentecost was fully come and there was a sound from heaven as of a rushing mighty wind. The apostles were not unprepared for a windy day; they were expecting the Spirit, 'spirit' and 'wind' were the same word, and Jesus had expressly linked the two (John 3:8).

The wind is invisible. It can only be known through the effects it produces – flags fluttering, trees swaying, seas rough and roaring, telephone wires singing, the door that bangs. But you can feel and know its power – buffeting you and blowing your hat off in its playful moods, but at other times flattening crops, uprooting trees, transforming calm seas into raging terrors.

Of this power our forefathers made much use – to get them across the ocean, pump water, grind corn. But we neglect it today because it's too chancy and unpredictable. Power we want, but it must be power we can control and rely on and switch on and off as we will. The wind is no use to us. It *blows where – and when – it wills, and you hear the sound of it, but you do not know whence it comes or whither it goes; so it is with every one who is born of the Spirit.*

The Holy Spirit is only known through the effects he produces: thoughts and deeds of love and holiness, words of unmistakable authority and inspiration. He speaks by the prophets and acts through the saints. And hearing and seeing such effects we begin to realize the immense power of the Spirit – mightily creative of good, but terrifyingly destructive of all that is false or flimsy.

Why do we not make more use of him? Because, like the wind, we cannot control him nor depend on him to get us where we have decided we want to go or to further our own plans and purposes. Dare we let him move us? Isn't it more sensible not to risk it, but play for safety?

But are we sure we really know what *safety* is – and how to play for it?

TRINITY SUNDAY

The Rainbow round the Throne

ONE of the glories of Winchester Cathedral is its great west window. It is not what it was. Nobody can say for certain what it was, though it has been suggested that when it was created by Thomas, the glazier appointed by William of Wykeham six centuries ago, its subject was the Coronation of the Virgin. In December 1642 it was smashed to pieces by Cromwellian soldiers. After the pillagers had left, the hundreds of fragments of broken glass were carefully gathered up, and when the King came to his own again at the Restoration they were put back as they are now – a great kaleidoscopic abstract through which the light pours with gleams and flashes of all the colours of the rainbow. Indeed, on a summer evening and with the setting sun behind it, it puts me in mind of that vision of that early Christian who, while interned on a Greek island, had the strange experience which he subsequently tried to put down on paper in what is now known as the Book of Revelation. He saw as it were a door open in heaven, and he heard a voice as it were a trumpet which told him to come up hither. And immediately he was in the spirit and 'there in heaven stood a throne, and on the throne sat one whose appearance was like the gleam of jasper and cornelian; and round about the throne there was a rainbow bright as an emerald' (Revelation 4:3).

It was an intensely colourful heaven into which St John was caught up – and there is something heavenly about all colour. Though often taken for granted, colour contributes much to our enjoyment of life in this world. Just think how much duller this world would be if everything were either black or white – no blue in sky or sea, no red in the sunset, no green in the grass, no gold in the ripe corn.

But now here is an odd fact: the Bible in general, and the New Testament in particular, is noticeably lacking in colour. There are, in the Authorized Version of the New Testament, over 180,000 words; but outside the Book of Revelation there are only twenty-seven words denoting colour. 'White' is the commonest; in one form or another it occurs just eight times; then comes purple – seven times; red, three times; black, three times; and two splashes each of gold, green, and scarlet. Of the two uses of the word 'green', however, one does not really denote colour at all, but translates a Greek word meaning 'full of sap'. The words 'brown' and 'yellow' and 'blue' never occur in the New Testament. Further, in almost every case such colour words as there are are used with reference to clothes; there are only two references to the colour of the landscape, only one to the colour of the sky, and none at all to the colour of the sea. It is not until we come to the Book of Revelation – written not in Palestine but on a Greek island – that the New Testament becomes at all colourful – and there is a rainbow round about the throne.

Why this lack of colour in holy Scripture – for what has been said of the New Testament is proportionately true of the Old Testament also? Three reasons may be suggested:

First, people in biblical times were simply not colour-conscious to the same extent as we are today – just as they were not much conscious of the natural beauty of the landscape. There was virtually no art of painting, and there is virtually no description of scenery in the Bible; people had no time to stop and stare, to notice and enjoy such things. The land meant hard work always, and danger often; it was thin pasture and scrubby hillside, stony field or battle field. Shepherds must watch their flocks by night and by day. If colour is noticed at all it is indoors, and particularly in clothing and precious stones – in Joseph's coat, in Solomon's glory, in the High Priest's breastplate, in the purple robe with which Jesus is dressed up by the Roman soldiery. For natural colour people had little eye.

Secondly: the climate of Palestine was – and is – such that the fresh natural colours of spring are quickly burnt up by the sun; thus the largely bald and stony countryside soon becomes, and for months remains, of a uniform, sun-scorched hue. There's no rich colourful summer, no golden autumn, no flaming fall. And that same heat which dries up the earth also dries up the air, so that there is none of that moisture-laden atmosphere which is so largely responsible for the brilliant colours of, say, the west of Scotland or of the Emerald Isle of Ireland.

The third, and perhaps the chief, reason why there is so little mention of colour in the Bible is the sheer all-pervading brightness of the light itself in the Holy Land. It was the intense luminosity of the sky above, and its hard, bright, sharp reflection off the surfaces of stone and rock on the earth beneath, which so impressed people – as it drained the landscape of its natural colours. This, rather than colours, was what they noticed – not the reds, yellows and blues of the spectrum, but the clear, brilliant radiance of the light itself – and, by contrast, the deep dark of shadow and cloud and night.

Now: it was that white intensity of the light itself through which the prophets and psalmists of Israel came to know so much of the nature of God, as it was through him who called himself 'the light of the world' that the writers of the New Testament came to know still more about him. Prophets and psalmists, apostles and evangelists – these were people of peculiar vision, who saw behind and beyond all outward appearance to the ultimate reality; who saw (as it were) behind and beyond all colour to what is, in reality, the source of all colour – the pure light itself. They were those who glimpsed, so to speak, beyond the rainbow round the throne to him who sitteth upon the throne.

So, from Genesis to Revelation, it is the testimony of such people that God is light, and in him is no darkness at all. He dwells in light unapproachable, says one. Clothed in majesty and honour, he decketh himself with light as with a garment, says another. This is the light which blazed out at the dawn of the creation and is said to be the source of all life; this is the light which Moses saw in a bush in the desert and which Isaiah glimpsed in the Temple – a light so bright that the seraphim must veil their faces. This is the light which Peter and James and John saw in Jesus when he was transfigured before them; the light which blinded Saul on the road to Damascus. This too is the sharp brilliance under which the world is judged, which pierces the darkness and reveals all things and all men for what they are, which makes all things new, which gives illumination to them that sit in darkness and in the shadow of death, and guides men's feet into the way of peace.

Of colour, I repeat, the Bible seems to have little — but on page after page of it the world of men is seen under the pure light which contains all colour, the blinding light of truth, the light which probes and pierces men and women, which quickens them into new life, which bathes them with serene radiance. Light is, as it were, the visual expression of the splendour and glory of God, of the perfect goodness of God, of the aweful holiness of God.

'Stop,' we cry, 'This is too much: we can't see all this.' It is too much. It is indeed. There have been many in the past, there are indeed men and women alive today, who have in fact experienced this illumination, and have seen all this in this light. It is a perfectly genuine and not uncommon mystical experience. But it is too much for the majority of us. As the hymn puts it, 'The eye of sinful man God's glory may not see.' It would kill most of us to see God now in all his naked and holy brilliance. We must have something between us and him, clouds and darkness round about him to temper the dazzle, a prism to split the glory of God into its myriad constituent colours. Even in heaven John saw a rainbow round about the throne.

And this is, in fact, how God in his mercy and understanding reveals himself to us — gleam by gleam, flash by flash, as precious stones splinter the light and give it to us gleam by gleam and flash by flash; as the great west window of Winchester Cathedral splinters the light and gives it to us in a sparkling kaleidoscopic diagram of all the colours of the rainbow. Once a year, on Trinity Sunday, we are to screw up our eyes to try to look for a blink into the heart of Light itself. But for the rest of the year, as the Sundays and weeks go by from Advent to Advent we are shown in the psalms, lessons, prayers, if we will but see them in the right way, one after another all the facets of God's being and activity in all their different colours — his power and imagination as Creator and Lord of History, his mercy and love in the life of Jesus, his sanctifying energy in the works of the Holy Spirit. And not only in our

94

services of worship but at all times and seasons we can see splinters and flashes of the glory of God in the loving, caring, understanding words and deeds of the men and women around us – in the words of their mouths, the looks in their eyes, in the smiles on their faces, in the touch of their hands. And inasmuch as the words of *your* mouth, the look in *your* eyes, the smile on *your* face and the touch of *your* hand can reflect just a splinter of the glory of God, *you* too are – or could be – part of the rainbow round about the throne.

But just once a year, on this particular day, Trinity Sunday, we are to screw up our eyes, our courage, our minds, our imaginations, and we are to peer through a glass darkly through the rainbow round the throne to try to descry upon that throne the source of all light and the heart of all colour – the ineffable being of God himself. We are, in faith, to acknowledge the glory of the eternal Trinity, and in the power of the divine Majesty to worship the Unity.

> Immortal, invisible, God only wise,
> In light inaccessible hid from our eyes,
> Most blessed, most glorious, the Ancient of Days,
> Almighty, victorious, thy great name we praise.

> Great Father of Glory, pure Father of light,
> Thine angels adore thee, all veiling their sight;
> All laud we would render: O help us to see
> 'Tis only the splendour of light hideth thee.

CORPUS CHRISTI

A Foretaste of Heaven

MANY are the references to eating and drinking in the Gospels. Jesus himself had something of a reputation in the matter, so that his critics accused him of being a gluttonous man and a winebibber. He attended banquets with the good and great, and likewise dined with publicans and sinners. Several of his parables have a feast as their setting. His feedings of the multitudes are recorded in all four Gospels. So is the Last Supper. At least two of his resurrection appearances are associated with meals.

Isaiah had written of a coming great day when the Lord would save his people, reestablish Jerusalem, and 'on this mountain the Lord of Hosts will prepare a banquet of rich fare for all the peoples …' (Isaiah 25:6). Many Jewish teachers subsequently developed and popularized this vision of God's redemption of man culminating in a heavenly banquet: as a fellow-guest with Jesus said at a dinner party, 'Blessed is he who shall eat bread in the Kingdom of God' (Luke 14:15).

It is that picture of the future, well-known to his contemporaries and keenly anticipated by them, which lay behind Jesus' parables about the Great Supper, the Wedding Feast and the return of the Prodigal Son. It was in his mind when he fed the multitudes, taught about the bread of life, and inaugurated the eucharist. And that rite is but half-appreciated if it is understood only as a memorial of Christ's saving acts in the past; it is also a foretaste of heaven.

Perhaps the loveliest personal expression of the idea in English is George Herbert's poem beginning:

> Love bade me welcome; yet my soul drew back,
> > Guilty of dust and sin.

To dine with God is something from which, like the Prodigal
Son, my penitent soul shrinks in shame ...

    'And know you not,' says Love, 'who bore the blame?'
      'My dear, then I will serve.'
    'You must sit down,' says Love, 'and taste my meat.'
      So I did sit and eat.

ST JOHN THE BAPTIST
(24th June)

Making Straight

As in earlier days and in different ways Saul and Jeremiah and Judas Maccabeus were men possessed – that is, men not entirely their own, but seized and taken over by something or someone else – so was John the Baptist. Indeed, some might say he never had a chance to be himself. The New Testament has it that from the moment of his conception he belonged to someone else, was already possessed, and at his naming his father said as much in that poetic utterance which the Church knows as the *Benedictus*. But it is true of us all that we never had a chance to be ourselves. From the beginning we belonged to, were possessed by, powers and persons outside ourselves – and what nonentities we should have been without them.

But Saul and Jeremiah and Judas Maccabeus and John the Baptist were persons who were, or who allowed themselves to be, possessed to a degree remarkable in their times by a remarkable power, the Holy Spirit of God. By that Spirit they were inspired to become exceptional men, that is, to do and say what otherwise they could not have done and said at that time.

It is especially true of John the Baptist that he was an exceptional man. Everything about him was out of the ordinary – even the food he ate and the way he dressed. The crowds who went out into the wilderness and down to the Jordan valley didn't go to contemplate the wind in the willows, or to gawp at celebrities dressed up for a royal occasion. They went to see a prophet who didn't mince his words, even about members of the royal family – something which ultimately cost him his life. And when people asked him who exactly he thought he was and what he was up to, his reply was extraordinary too: he said he was a voice crying in the wilderness 'Make straight the way of the Lord.' He said he was a *voice* – that is, nothing to look at but something to listen to, something for which you needed your ears, not your eyes. And what that voice cried was 'Make straight the way of the Lord.'

John was, of course, quoting an earlier prophet, but he was also defining his own function. He was, he claimed, that very person whom Isaiah had said would be sent on ahead to clear the road and make it ready for the approaching king. John's job was to level that road, remove all its obstructions – and above all make it straight. What sort of a road was this, and where did it lead? Where was the king going to establish his kingdom? When the King came, he answered the question himself, like this: 'The Kingdom of God is within you.' And therefore the way that John had to prepare was a way into the hearts and souls of men and women. 'To that end,' cried John, 'repent, mend your ways, and demonstrate that you are a new person by washing off the old in this river. You who are well-to-do, share your possessions with those in need. You whose job it is to collect rents and rates and fees and taxes, exact no more than is proper. You soldiers, behave yourselves, and stop looting. And you, Herod, leave your brother's wife alone.' In all that John was saying 'Make straight the way of the Lord.'

Make straight. 'The straight line and the right angle,' said the archaeologist F. J. Haverfield, '... are the marks which sunder even the simplest civilization from barbarism.' Since then the researches of other scholars in various fields have confirmed the truth of Haverfield's judgement, and shown that straightness is an almost universal symbol of what is right and good, as crookedness is a symbol of what is wrong and evil. In primitive art, straight lines, right angles, squares, circles, perfect curves – all these appear to denote orderliness, regularity, that which is good. Twisty lines, on the other hand, and irregular shapes, and lines that are blurred and indistinct – these denote the unknown, the unpredictable, the unfriendly, the chaotic, that which is evil. And so it is that in many of the world's great myths and fairy tales the hero is a tall, straight, square-shouldered man who, whatever his origins and misfortunes, triumphs over every evil and is, at the end of the story, living happily ever after in a royal palace of battlemented walls, square towers, rectangular courtyards, formal gardens. The villain, on the contrary, is a misshapen ogre or dwarf or hunchback who lives in the depths of a trackless forest among the gnarled trunks and twisting roots of the trees, a deformed creature who has his lair in the centre of a maze of twisting tunnels, like the Minotaur in the labyrinth or Tolkien's Gollum in a cave beneath the mountains. Or look at a picture of St George and the dragon: the saint upright and erect, thrusting a dead-straight spear into the jaws of the writhing dragon about which there is nothing straight at all – its body bent, its legs bandy, its tail coiled, twists of flame and smoke curling from its nostrils.

Turn to the Bible, and the symbolism is similar. From beginning to end God is represented as a Being of order and regularity. When he creates the universe he brings order out of chaos, appoints regular courses for the heavenly bodies, and his whole work of creation follows an orderly sequence. When he tells Noah to build an ark, or Moses to make a tabernacle, he gives precise measurements – and the result in each case is a perfectly symmetrical construction. And when the author of the Book of Revelation sees in a vision the heavenly city, new Jerusalem, what he sees is a perfectly planned city with four-square walls.

Babylon, or Babel, on the other hand, is the shapeless, sprawling city of disorder and confusion ruled by a devil who is a creature of twist and turns, and who can never be trusted because he is completely unpredictable and governed by neither law nor order. The tempter is one thing one moment and something else the next, and always pretending to be something other than he is. He is the arch-hypocrite, slithering his way like a worm into the minds and souls of men and women, equally master of the art of camouflage and of the art of ventriloquism. In Genesis he is represented as a smooth and slippery serpent, in the Book of Revelation as a scaly dragon. It is not without significance that when John the Baptist told his hearers to make straight the way of the Lord he called them 'the offspring of vipers', little reptiles.

And all this is reflected in our idomatic English speech, so that the word 'straight' has two principal meanings. There is the original and (so to say) mathematical meaning, as when we speak of a straight line, a straight road, or a cricketer playing with a straight bat. But there is also the metaphorical and moral sense, where 'straight' means orderly, honest, sincere, truthful, just. So we speak of straightforwardness, of straight dealing, of straight speaking, of people 'keeping straight' and 'going straight'. In a similar way we speak of a man being upright, and such a man is not ashamed of being called 'square'. You may feel inclined to sneer at him, but (bless him) he can always be trusted to give you a square deal.

On the other hand, where dishonesty is suspected, it is said that so and so is 'not quite straight'. If we want to be polite we may say that he is a bit devious, that he 'follows a tortuous course'. More outspokenly we may call him a bit of a twister; and if he be manifestly criminal, then he is vulgarly and vividly known as a crook.

All this helps us to understand what John the Baptist was seized of, what that possessed man was getting at when he said he was only a voice, but a voice crying 'Make straight the way of the Lord.' The Lord himself was about to come to establish his kingdom of Love, and John was as nothing compared to him, scarcely fit to clean his boots; but how far the Lord of Love would get, and how long the final establishment of his kingdom would take, would depend upon how far people were ready for him. For love has a hard time of it where there is mistrust and insincerity and lawlessness; love has a hard time of it where deeds and words and thoughts are crooked.

And such is the tendency of our mortal nature to go crooked, to prefer pliant expediency to straight principle, that John the Baptist's cry has still to be broadcast. We are continually being tempted to be not quite straight in our dealing if we think we can profitably and safely get away with it; not quite straight in our speaking if we think it will win us the approval of those whose good opinion we are anxious to win; not quite straight in our thinking if we find that straight thinking is leading us to unpleasant and uncomfortable conclusions.

Worse than that: such is our tendency to deviate from the straight and true that we often find it very difficult to know what is straight and true. If you have a line on a piece of paper and want to test whether or not it is straight, you lay along it a straight edge, a ruler. And so the rules and laws which society has evolved fulfil an important function in helping us to keep straight, or at least in indicating what is not straight. But the value of the rule of law is strictly limited. It is itself the work of human minds subject to the same inherent tendency to deviate from the straight; and since law is only concerned with the relations of human beings in society, it does not help individuals in many of their private problems. Such individuals must then fall back on their consciences. But even consciences can be horribly twisted. Remembering some of the deeds that have been perpetrated in the name of conscience, someone might well despair of making straight the way of the Lord if he has no more reliable ruler than that.

But as Christians we believe that we have been given one fault-less straight edge, one perfect and utterly reliable ruler: God himself revealed in human terms in the person of Jesus, our Christ and our King. We do well to pray from time to time that old collect from the *Book of Common Prayer* 'that thou being our ruler and guide we may so pass through things temporal that we finally lose not the things eternal'.

Make straight the way of the Lord.

AFTER TRINITY

Gardens

Garden Paths to God

To be led up the garden path is to be led astray. We owe this proverbial phrase to the Serpent. But if it is God and not Satan who leads, the path will bring us to nothing but good. And most of us will find such a path congenial, for we are garden-lovers at heart; no less than 85% of Britain's householders have a garden. It is almost instinctive to tend the plots of earth around our homes and cherish the plants we choose to grow in them. No trivial part of inner city misery is being deprived of the chance to satisfy that instinct, and ingenious are the ways in which dwellers in blocks of flats – and those no longer physically capable of gardening – find substitutes in window-boxes and pots of plants.

Our love of gardens is reflected in the Bible which begins with a garden and ends with a garden-city. Other familiar biblical gardens are the Garden of Gethsemane and that in which Jesus was buried and where Mary Magdalene met him after his resurrection. There was Naboth's vineyard which Ahab coveted for his own herb garden (1 Kings 21:2); the garden which God would make of the desert (Isaiah 35); the great garden described in Ecclesiastes (2:4–5); the garden repeatedly referred to in the Song of Solomon. At least one of the parables of Jesus concerns a garden problem (Luke 13:6–9), and others make a direct appeal to gardeners as well as farmers. And throughout both Testaments there are many references to garden work – digging, dunging, sowing, planting, weeding, staking, pruning and so on.

Many religious writers in post-biblical times have found gardens fertile ground for all manner of symbols with which to illustrate their teaching. Just how luxuriant a garden the Christian imagination can become may be gauged from the fact that St Bernard wrote no less than eighty sermons on the first two chapters of the Song of Solomon and its garden! Limited space prevents such exuberance of fancy in these meditations, but there is certainly a theme here which God can use to feed our thinking and praying.

Ruminate on these words of Paul for a start: 'You are God's garden' (1 Corinthians 3:9).

The Office of a Wall

As a garden, 'this other Eden, demi-paradise' – so Shakespeare saw England; and went on to stress the importance to 'this blessed plot' of the surrounding sea 'which serves it in the office of a wall'.

A wall – or a moat, hedge or ha-ha – is essential to a garden. No horticulture can begin until there is a fence of some kind to define the area to be cultivated. The English *garden*, French *jardin*, German *garten* are related to the old English *garth* and *yard*; the Romans had their *hortus* and the Greeks their *chortos* – relatives again of our *court* and *orchard*; and every one of those words had as its original meaning an enclosure beside a house.

It was the same in Hebrew: the word translated *garden* in the Bible was derived from a verb meaning to fence – which explains why hedges or walls are often specifically mentioned in connection with biblical gardens and vineyards (e.g. Psalm 80:12, Isaiah 5:5, Mark 12:1), as are the walls of the garden city of New Jerusalem (Revelation 21).

The office of the wall is to demark 'the blessed plot' which the gardener intends to cultivate, and to separate it from the formless wilderness and chaos outside. More than that, the wall helps to defend the garden from all manner of forces – winds, weeds, wild beasts – which, unless kept at bay, will stunt, overwhelm and finally destroy the special plants the gardener wants to grow.

'Something there is that doesn't love a wall' (Robert Frost, *Mending Wall*) – and that is particularly true today. Many are crying loud and long for the levelling and demolition of all that distinguishes and divides man from man. When the walls and barriers in question are obstacles to proper growth – like Chesterton's walls of gold which entomb us – then Christians should be in the forefront of the assault upon them. But when, like the Ten Commandments, they stand between society and anarchy, man and chaos, humanity and inhumanity, and are needed to protect our freedom to grow and become what, by the grace of God, we have it in us to become – then it is madness and murder to let them crumble.

A Watered Garden

IF a garden cannot properly begin without a wall or hedge to define it, so it cannot continue without fresh waters to give it life. In Britain there is always the rain, but in the hotter drier lands in the East where horticulture began every garden is a 'watered garden' with streams, channels, fountains and pools. So:

> In Xanadu did Kubla Khan
>   A stately pleasure-dome decree:
> Where Alph, the sacred river, ran
> Through caverns measureless to man ...
> And here were gardens bright with sinuous rills

– and 'a mighty fountain', and the sacred river 'five miles meandering with a mazy motion'. Coleridge's picture and all such paradises have their archetype in Genesis where a river flowed out of Eden to water the garden and there it divided and became four rivers embracing and giving life to the whole known world (Genesis 2:10–14). Those living waters run right through the Holy Scriptures and are seen in particular in Ezekiel 47:1–12 and Revelation 22:1–3.

The source of the waters of life is expressly located by Jesus as being in himself, and the waters are the Holy Spirit: 'If any man thirst, let him come to me and drink. He that believes in me, as scripture says, out of his heart shall flow rivers of living water' – and the evangelist explains: 'This he said of the Spirit.' One of the passages which Jesus had in mind was doubtless Isaiah 58:11, where the prophet speaks of how God will satisfy his people with good things so that they shall be 'like a watered garden'.

But we live in an age of spiritual drought and in a world of religious deserts – and 'the desert is within you' (T. S. Eliot). In the prayer life of many of our individual selves, not to mention the world at large, there are all sorts of tell-tale signs of drought: good soil reduced to dust, dying trees, dry stems, shrivelled buds, leaves and flowers and fruits all desiccated – and no bird sings. All of which suggests that we do not pray as we should, for God never fails to give the Holy Spirit to those who ask (Luke 11:13).

Under the Trees

A garden may have its walls and waters, but it will still not be what biblical writers understood by a garden unless it has trees. In the description of God planting a 'paradise of delice' (Wyclif's translation) eastward in Eden there is no mention of flowers; the important fact is that 'the Lord God made to grow in it every tree that is pleasant to the sight and good for food'.

Quite apart from their fruit and beauty, trees are essential to a garden for the shade they provide. To this day, in the hot lands of the Middle East and the Mediterranean, the most valued feature of even the smallest garden is that carefully tended tree beside the house under which the household gather to rest and refresh themselves in the middle of the day, finding a deep, cool delight in the shade which shields them from the sun's heat and the noon's blinding glare. And it is under that tree that, at the day's end, they relax and enjoy again a sense of homely security. The prophet Micah (4:4) wrote of a day when swords would be beaten into ploughshares and nations learn war no more, 'but they shall sit every man under his vine and under his fig tree' – as in the golden days of Solomon (1 Kings 4:25).

If the Church is God's garden, as Paul put it, what are the 'trees' under which we may rest and refresh ourselves from time to time before going on our way through the world and back to our work in the vineyard? One kind of 'tree' is represented by places of worship; it is in our praying, both together and by ourselves, that we can find deep and reviving shade.

There are also particular men and women we know who, through the goodness, grace and stability of their Christian lives, are 'like trees planted by the waterside' (Psalm 1:1–4) and in whose presence we always find peace and healing after the glare and heat of the busy world. Should we not think of ourselves as planted by God to give such shade to others?

Above all, there is Him who said: 'I am the true vine' (John 15:1).

Consider the Lilies

WHILE a garden means flowers to most of us, the gardeners of the Bible had little time or space for flowers. All their energies went into creating coolness and shade and growing plants for food and medicinal purposes. They had no leisure to cultivate flowers for their own sake, and (with the exception of those in 'the garden enclosed' of the Song of Solomon) virtually all the flowers of the Bible are wild flowers.

Not that people were oblivious of the beauty of flowers. They doubtless appreciated (though rarely mentioned) their colours; they certainly enjoyed their scents; above all they appreciated the beauty of what James called 'the grace of the fashion' of them (James 1:11) and it was the loveliness of flower shapes which led to their being used for decorative purposes (e.g. Exodus 25:31; 1 Kings 7:26).

The best known example of the appreciation of the beauty of flowers is in Jesus' teaching his followers to consider the lilies of the field which surpass in loveliness even Solomon in all his glory (Matthew 6:28–30). But brief is that beauty – it's gone tomorrow, burnt up by sun and scorching wind or cut down by the man with the scythe.

It is that transitoriness of flowers that it noticed repeatedly – by Job, the Psalmist, Isaiah, James and Peter as well as by Jesus – and the point is made that in the brevity of their flowering they resemble man himself whose 'days are but as grass: for he flourisheth as a flower of the field. For as soon as the wind goeth over it, it is gone; and the place thereof shall know it no more. But the merciful goodness of the Lord endureth for ever and ever upon them that fear him' (Psalm 103:15–17).

To many it is tragic that such loveliness should perish so quickly. But the person of faith is not dismayed. Such a one knows there can be no seed, no fruit, no flowers next year – no resurrection – if this year's petals hang on and don't drop. So we pray in the old collect for the fourth Sunday after Trinity that God will increase and multiply upon his mercy 'that we may so pass through things temporal that we finally lose not the things eternal'.

Planting

What God first did eastward in Eden was to 'plant' – first man, then trees; that is, he set young lives in a prepared environment where they could grow into what, by his gift, they had it in them to become. And to this day a gardener's basic work is that setting of plants, slips and seedlings in appointed places where their roots may reach out freely, and their stems grow up in light and air and come to flower and fruit.

It is a work involving several processes: first, deep and strong spadework to turn and break up the ground; then the actual setting of the plants in the soil thus prepared, an operation requiring a sensitive combination of gentleness and firmness (for green fingers don't grow on heavy hands, but young plants not settled firmly wilt and weaken); and then there is the watering to help them settle in.

The planting metaphor appears throughout the Bible. As God planted his garden in Eden so he planted his people in the Promised Land (Psalm 80:8–11). Jesus employed the metaphor (e.g. Matthew 15:13, 21:33) and Paul used it to describe the foundation of the Church in Corinth – he had done the planting, Apollos the watering. From that it is a short step to see baptism as the planting of a human being in God's garden, the beginning of his or her spiritual growth; and 'such as are planted in the house of the Lord shall flourish in the courts of the house of our God' (Psalm 92:12).

This reminds us that those who are members of a church have certain responsibilities when a new member comes to be baptized. It is up to us, on the human level, to see that the soil is in as good a condition as we can make it, that the new member is given a grounding both sensitive and firm, and then well watered in.

Not that we should pride ourselves if 'our sons grow up as the young plants' (Psalm 144:12) to the glory of God. We have only been dutiful under-gardeners. Paul planted, Apollos watered, but 'God gave the increase' (1 Corinthians 3:6).

The Use of the Knife

To take a knife to a healthy growing plant and deliberately amputate it is not, on the face of it, a kind or sensible thing to do. That prehistoric man who first pruned a tree may well have been thought mad if not brutal by his fellows; but he was observant, and had probably noticed the surprisingly beneficial consequences – stronger growth and greater fruitfulness – which had followed the dismembering of a tree by a freak gust of wind or some other accident.

What is certain is that, long before Christ's day, the practice of pruning was well understood as an essential operation of good husbandry (e.g. Isaiah 2:4; 5:6), and, in a passage of which every phrase should be pondered, Jesus himself spoke of pruning with reference to himself and the Church: 'I am the real vine, and my Father is the gardener. Every barren branch of mine he cuts away; and every fruiting branch he cleans, to make it more fruitful still. You have already been cleansed by the word that I spoke to you' (John 15:1–2). In the characteristically florid language of a late seventeenth-century divine: 'The great Husbandman of Souls takes this Course with his spiritual Vines, to add the Pruning-hook of his Judgements to the more general Manurings of his Mercy' (Robert South).

The good gardener, following the great Husbandman, knows that whatever is weakening a tree, or hindering it from attaining the full beauty and fruitfulness of which it is capable, is best cut out – but always with wisdom, understanding and complete control. The knife must be clean and sharp, applied in the right place and at the right season, and always with a surgeon's precision.

Sometimes such treatment may seem, as it seemed to Job, harsh and unfair, merciless and cruel – particularly when it is ourselves or those closest to us who are subjected to the discipline of pruning that we may the more generously bring forth the fruits of the Spirit. We should remember the incalculably fruitful consequences of Christ submitting himself to be stripped and crucified, and pray with Jeremiah 'O Lord, correct me, but with judgement; not in thine anger, lest thou bring me to nothing' (Jeremiah 10:24).

Garden and Desert

THOUGH not Paradise by a long chalk, it had the vestiges of it: a stream-bed nearby which was sometimes full of water, a wall round it, and a depth of that cool silver-green shade which only olives can give (its name, Gethsemane, implies there had once been an olive press there). And, as God had liked to walk in Paradise in the cool of the evening (Genesis 3:8) so Jesus often resorted there (John 18:1–2). It had little appeal to those who revelled in the garish noise, jostle and excitement of city streets. But Jesus found stillness there. It was a place you could pray in.

It was also like Eden – and places of prayer – in that creatures of subtlety could find a way in, making it a place of excruciating temptation and a setting for weakness and disloyalty, so that the second Adam, though as strong as the first had been weak, was there 'betrayed and given up into the hands of wicked men' who led him away from the garden and all that it meant into the courts of men in the city – and, on the following morning, into an open space the other side of the city.

That space was no Eden – just a desert, a bald mound, skull-shaped and lacking everything that makes a garden: unwalled, devoted not to the growing of living things but to their destruction, and open to that public which has little interest in the beauty and sweetness of flower and fruit but finds the spice of life in watching spectacles of violence, cruelty and blood. No water there, no shade, no trees.

That's not wholly true. Three trees were planted there that same morning, and on one of them he who had called himself the true vine, after being savagely pruned and stripped naked, was spreadeagled, fixed, lifted up and left exposed to the full flame of the sun and the eyes of all who wanted to watch. Unless you were put in mind of a scarecrow, the place was as far from a garden as you could imagine. It was more like a rubbish dump and desert – which is what sinful human beings have made, and still make, of the garden in which God has placed them.

Paradise Regained

'Now in the place where he was crucified,' John was careful to write, 'there was a garden, and in the garden a new tomb' (John 19:41). There the body of Jesus was laid, and there on the third day the new creation began – in a quiet, secluded corner of that otherwise desolate space where the only trees were crosses. Out of the dark death of the earth in that corner new life appeared – as Isaiah had foretold: 'The wilderness and the solitary place shall be glad, and the desert shall rejoice and blossom as the rose' (Isaiah 35:1).

Among the first given the opportunity to know that spring had arrived was Mary Magdalene. But it took her by surprise – as we are surprised by the first snowdrop – indeed, she didn't even see it at first. To her, the world was still all winter, so dark and cold and hard it was. The very place in which the body of her adored Master had been buried was empty, so that she had nothing to look forward to, not even a grave to visit. She could only look back to summer days that were gone. All that remained was a blank hole – and not so much as a bunch of withered flowers for a keepsake.

So when Jesus met her she supposed him to be the gardener (John 20:14). When your eyes are full of tears, and all your feelings and attention drowned in what has been, it is not surprising if you don't notice what is; still less surprising if you can't see what will be. So she didn't recognize the first sign of spring; she only supposed him to be the gardener.

In all innocence she supposed the precise truth. That is who he was. The second Adam was at work regaining the Paradise that the first had lost. And his work still goes on, for gardens take some making – and something of what is involved we have pondered in these meditations.

And the end? Not just a garden, but that garden-city John glimpsed with its walls, water and trees (Revelation 21–22:5). Blessed are they who find themselves planted therein to give, by the beauty of the flowering of their personalities, eternal glory and joy to the Gardener.

115

Being in Love

> Jacob served seven years for Rachel; and they seemed unto him but a few days for the love he had to her. (Genesis 29:20)

> Love is of God: and everyone that loveth is born of God, and knoweth God. He that loveth not knoweth not God; for God is love. (1 John 4:7–8)

Jacob has learned a thing or two. Two chapters back in Genesis he was a smooth, crafty little man without a heart in his body. His only concern was for himself and his prospects, and he preferred to live by the sharpness of his wits rather than by honest work. His brother dutifully went hunting for the wherewithal to make the savoury meat his father had asked for; Jacob took a short cut, snitched two good kids from his father's flock, and then proceeded to deceive the blind old man with a trick that was as mean as it was original. He thus stole from his brother the blessing that should have been his, and the only qualm Jacob had was that he might be found out.

But that was two chapters back, and since then Jacob has twice had a glimpse of heaven. And those two glimpses have made all the difference. We now see that he has a heart after all. He falls in love with a girl at first sight, puts himself out to remove the stone from the well and waters her flocks for her. He kisses her, and so full of love is his heart that he weeps for joy, and willingly binds himself to work seven years for her father that he may have her as his bride at the end. 'And they seemed unto him but a few days, for the love he had to her.' It is indeed a very changed Jacob, due it would seem to the fact that (as I put it just now) he has twice had a glimpse of heaven since he fled from home with the blessing he had snatched. The first time he looked into heaven was in a dream, the dream of the ladder. The second time he looked into heaven was when he looked into Rachel's eyes.

I choose those words deliberately. For I believe that to fall in love is to have a foretaste of heaven, and that the experience of falling in love can tell us something about the love of God for

116

ourselves and about the love we should have for him. But I must beware. It is dangerously easy to be appallingly unreal where God and love are concerned. We are continually being told that God loves us, and that we should love him — but what does it all mean? With the word 'love' we are exceedingly familiar, but most of the things with which the word is commonly associated in our minds seem to have little to do with the faith and practice of supernatural religion. And many people are so inclined to be embarrassed or sentimental or silly about 'love' that when they hear Scripture speaking of the Church as 'the bride of Christ' the idea strikes them as being really rather extravagant and ridiculous, and not quite in the best of taste.

If to any extent we share such opinions, then the fault is partly in ourselves in so far as we have allowed the novels and newspapers we read, and the plays and films we see, to bamboozle us into thinking of love solely in terms of sex, and of sex solely in terms of getting into bed with someone. But partly the fault is in the theologians and preachers who, in their anxiety to emphasize that divine love is not like human love in *that* respect, have tended to suggest that it is not like human love in any respect. So they have explained that the word in Greek doesn't mean what you think it means; they have called it 'charity'; they have labelled it a 'theological virtue'; and they have written, composed and preached innumerable books and hymns, anthems and sermons on the subject, leaving the ordinary man and woman with the vague notion that it's all very wonderful and beautiful, no doubt, but too cold and bloodless by half, and only for saints and other religious specialists.

But there is much in the Bible, and not least in the New Testament, to suggest that human love and divine love have not a little in common. The writers of the Scriptures were neither shy nor ashamed to use the former as an image for the latter — to describe the Day of the Lord, for instance, in terms of a marriage between God and his people, to call Christ a bridegroom and the Church his bride. And perhaps you have noticed that Jesus himself was particularly fond of using weddings as subjects for his parables. St John was only summing up a whole strand in the Bible's teaching when he wrote: 'Love is of God; and everyone that loveth is born of God, and knoweth God. He that loveth not knoweth not God; for God is love.'

So I hope you will take it from me, if you haven't already discovered the truth for yourself, that when a boy and girl fall in love and tell each other that they're 'in heaven', there's more in what they say than is commonly allowed. They are 'in heaven', they say. Time doesn't count, and all is joy and ecstasy. True, the ecstasy may soon vanish – it does not usually last indefinitely in this world. God, perhaps, withdraws the vision, and the lover begins to see that the beloved is only human after all, and has his or her own faults just like every other human. But that in no way invalidates the truth, or destroys the reality, of the first vision. Lovers *have* seen heaven in each other's faces. But God may then withdraw the vision, and leave them to work hard both to recapture it in this life, and to be worthy of heaven hereafter, heaven where the vision becomes the reality and all are 'in love' for ever. That, indeed, is a definition of heaven worth consideration – the state of 'being in love' for ever. And for that reason, let no Christian ever be guilty of that blasphemy which regards the ecstasy of two lovers with a cynical indifference, or as a fit topic for tittle-tattle, or as subject-matter for a slimy joke. Whenever we see this love in the faces of lovers, let us rejoice; let us smile with them, not gossip about them, still less laugh at them. And let us, if the experience has ever been granted to us, recall those heavenly days when we too enjoyed a similar ecstasy. That vision may have vanished long ago – but that should not occasion surprise, still less cynicism; for this earth, after all, is not heaven. But this earth will one day pass away and there will be no more sea – and then woe to that man or woman who thinks of being in love, being in heaven, with cynical indifference, as no more than suitable matter for teacup tittle-tattle or a patronizing jest.

Let me now go further and attempt (with appalling rashness and inadequacy) a cold and concise analysis of the state of being in love, and to suggest what can be learned from it about the love of God for us and about our love for him.

It is all to be summed up by the one word *adoration* – and adoration begins, of course, with a vision, when the lover sees in another something of no ordinary grace and goodness and beauty: some quality that today might be called 'fabulous', but which yesterday would have been described more appropriately as 'out of this world'. And this vision of unearthly loveliness not merely attracts him but sets his heart on fire – and makes him feel strangely small. The true lover is utterly humble in the presence of the beloved. If he thinks of himself at all, it is only to feel how wretchedly unworthy he is; he can scarcely believe his good luck should his beloved so much as notice him. And then, sooner or later, there will be a direct and courageous statement of what is going on in his heart – courageous because it is an act of faith, a burning of boats, and may lead at least to a slap in the face, and possibly to the total destruction of all hope. But such is his love that the act of faith must be made; Jacob, having put the lid on the well, turns round, risks all – and kisses Rachel. Sooner or later, when opportunity offers or is contrived, the boy breaks the ice and tells the girl he loves her – and why, because she is so this and so that. Very often, if the poets are right, he says in so many words that he sees heaven in her eyes, her smile, or whatever it is.

Vision, humility, faith – and then in adoration there is obedience. The beloved has but to command, and the lover will give all to obey. He – or of course she – is not merely ready but anxious to give delight and to demonstrate his or her devotion by serving the beloved. So to obey is in no way a distasteful duty, or, indeed, a duty at all; it is a joyous privilege. To think that she has actually asked him to do something for her! He says – and he means it – 'I will do anything for you, darling.' So Jacob served seven years for Rachel.

And lastly, if the beloved returns the love (which may not necessarily be the case) then the lover will *gladly accept* that love, so that between two lovers there is a complete exchange of adoration: each is humble enough to give all *and* each is humble enough to receive all. There is, in such a relationship, none of that servile abasement which freely offers everything – and flatly refuses to accept anything in return.

Such, then, are some of the qualities which, compounded together, make up the state of adoration, of being in love: a vision of no ordinary loveliness, humility, courageous faith, total obedience, and a readiness to receive as well as to give. Now, what shall we say are the effects of being in love on a person? Again there is only time for the merest sketch of an answer, but it would appear that these are some of the things most lovers experience.

First and foremost: an overall, general feeling of – happiness is too weak a word – say rather a thrilling ecstasy, an exaltation of the spirit which makes two lovers want to sing and to join in the dance of the whole creation with which they feel themselves to be so much in step.

For that, too, is part of the experience – a new sense of significance and right proportion: all things seem to fall into place; there is a feeling that all things are working together for good; good things seem better, bad things not so bad as they were. Lovers are aware of new glory everywhere. Even a grey, wet day is not so depressing if it means they can be together, for the world seen through their eyes is a brighter world. Everything lights up, their senses are heightened; the very flowers seem brighter, the songs of birds more piercingly lovely. Sir Osbert Sitwell has confessed somewhere that until he first fell in love he had been, as it were, *colourblind*.

And further: such is their sense that all things are working together for good that lovers have a great feeling of goodwill towards others; their love, as it were, overflows; they cannot help being generous. In the event, this is often the first thing to disappear, either because the lovers themselves become so selfishly wrapped up in each other that they only see other people as intruders – or, perhaps, because a clumsy lack of understanding and sensibility in others causes them to shut down like limpets.

And, too, there comes to those in love a new sense of peace and contentment: so long as they are together, let the skies fall, they do not care. And let the clocks strike, they do not care. Clocks tell the time, but those in love are in a measure outside time, in touch with something eternal – and that is the ground of their peace and contentment. Jacob served seven years for

Rachel; and they seemed unto him but a few days, for the love he had to her.

Now, with all that in mind, let us see briefly what it suggests to us about God's love for us and ours for him. That he loves us the Christian is unable to doubt — though he may well wonder what on earth God can see in him that is at all lovable. Still, the Gospels are there for us all to read, and what they tell us of all that Jesus did and suffered is a measure of God's love for us. And if we have ever really appreciated the sheer out-of-this-world goodness of Jesus, it must set our hearts on fire — and make us feel strangely small. That will be the basic quality of our love for God — utter humility. But that must lead on, sooner or later, to a direct and courageous confession of faith, and we shall tell him of our love. We need have no fear of the consequences in this case — but he has done all he can, and it is now for us to make a move on our side, to tell him we love him, and why. That is what prayer is — or should be — a converse between lovers. And it will lead on to an anxiety to obey and serve him, to do anything for him, and not for seven years only. But such obedience will never seem a duty. To think that God should ever be so gracious as to ask you or me to do anything for him! It is a privilege to obey! So, too, while he who loves God is humble enough to give all, so he is humble enough to accept all, all the gifts and graces God wants us to have, and not least those he extends to us in the sacraments.

And if we will thus be in love with God as he is with us, what follows?

A new and thrilling exaltation of the spirit which almost compels us to sing and rejoice. And our joy is infectious, so that we overflow with goodwill towards all our fellows. All things fall into place, and everything begins to make sense. Those who truly love God have a vivid sense of God's glory all about them; they see the world not as something drab and grey, but as the beautiful and sparkling thing it is, even when men hurl their horrors and hatreds all over it, even when the earth shakes and the rocks are rent and a city is thereby laid in ruins. I do not dare to boast that I have such a love for God, but this is surely the testimony of all the saints: that

those who love God know a peace and joy which pass our understanding. St Paul sat in chains in Philippi, *singing*, while the earthquake rocked his gaol. So let the skies fall, it will make no
difference; for if someone loves God he has, even now, a sense that
time does not matter, or rather, that eternity is already about him
— so that, for instance, increasing age or the approach of death do
not daunt, for what is death but the gateway to that heaven where
all are in love for ever? It may very well be that much has to be
endured — weeks, months, years, of earthly toil and difficulty and
pain and grief — but he who knows that God loves him, and
himself returns that love, quietly endures it all. He experiences
something akin to what Jacob experienced when he served seven
years for Rachel: they seemed unto him but a few days, for the
love he had to her.

> For love is of God; and everyone that loveth is born of God,
> and knoweth God. He that loveth not knoweth not God; for
> God is love.

The Sea

Beside the Seaside

JESUS was often on the beach. There he called disciples, taught and fed crowds, healed the sick, cast out devils. Later on, after he himself had gone down into the abyss of death and risen to life again the third day, one of his most fully reported appearances took place on the edge of the Sea of Tiberias. The disciples had spent a fruitless night fishing, but 'morning came, and there stood Jesus on the beach' (John 21:4) – and it is beside the seaside that the author leaves Jesus with us at the end of the fourth Gospel.

There are doubtless a number of humdrum, rational explanations to account for Jesus being so often on the seashore. But poets and prophets and the various authors of, for example, *The Odyssey*, *The Divine Comedy*, *The Tempest* and *Moby Dick* would see the beach as something more than a convenient spot for mass-meetings. The shore is significant because it is the frontier between two totally different elements. There land meets sea, solid meets fluid; the fixity and stillness of *terra firma* are opposed to the ceaseless movement and sound of water. One way leads to the heights, the other to the depths.

And that is our human situation. We live in a frontier region between nature and supernature, between flesh and spirit, in a narrow strip which is both the coast of heaven and the edge of the abyss. And while we rightly think of the earth as our element, those who live on an island, as most of us do, are never wholly forgetful of the great waters that surround us and their deep significance for us.

It will be the object of the following meditations to consider the sea and something of its significance for the religious spirit. 'They that go down to the sea in ships and occupy their business in great waters: these men see the works of the Lord and his wonders in the deep' (Psalm 107:23–24) – but the most seasoned land dweller should not miss the significance of the fact that Jesus deliberately chose to teach a great multitude when it was 'by the sea on the land' (Mark 4:1).

The Wide, Wide Sea

THE Old Testament writers used two very different words for what we should generally call the sea, and the makers of the Authorized Version were careful to retain the distinction, employing 'sea' for one and 'the deep' for the other. Again, the New Testament writers used the one word sea for both the Mediterranean and the inland lake of Galilee. But more of that later. For the moment it is enough to recall that one of the fundamental things the sea meant to the Israelites was an expanse of water sufficiently wide for waves to be formed; the commonest Hebrew word for it had at its root the idea of roaring – from the characteristic sound of its breaking on the shore.

The sheer wideness of the sea, a heaving expanse of water as far as the eye could reach, must have been an awesome sight to the nomadic Israelites when they first came to it from the inland grazing grounds to which they were accustomed – and it was nothing less than terrible to Coleridge's Ancient Mariner who found himself 'alone on a wide, wide sea'. That vastness impressed the Psalmist: 'the earth is full of thy riches,' he sang to God – and went on: 'So is the great and wide sea also' (Psalm 104:25). The creator of such an immensity of waters must be majestic indeed.

But Old Testament writers came to know that the greatness of God was so wide that it included very much more than his majestic creative powers, 'for as his majesty is, so also is his mercy' (Ecclesiasticus 2:18) and 'many waters cannot quench love' (Song of Songs 8:7). And this led F. W. Faber, the Victorian hymn writer, to compose some lines worth our taking to heart:

> There's a wideness in God's mercy,
> Like the wideness of the sea ...
>
> For the love of God is broader
> Than the measures of man's mind;
> And the heart of the Eternal
> Is most wonderfully kind.

But we make his love too narrow
By false limits of our own;
And we magnify his strictness
With a zeal he will not own.

The Monstrous Sea

LOCH Ness is not the only deep to have its monster. In many parts of the world people have had their folk-tales of the dark chaotic depths of the sea being the domains of monsters – usually a sea-serpent or dragon – who swallow up human beings whenever they can. The Greeks had their myth of Perseus rescuing Andromeda from such a beast, and our own ancestors in North Europe had their story of the monster which emerged from the depths to prey upon humans until it was slain by Beowulf in the heart of the abyss where it lived. It is easy to understand how people came to imagine such things when they had seen the sea thrashed into a destructive welter, their coasts battered, men and ships engulfed and sunk without trace.

Such myths were current in the ancient Middle East and there are many references in the Bible to such sea monsters (e.g. Job 7:12; Psalm 74:13–14; Isaiah 27:1) variously called Leviathan, Rahab, serpent, dragon, beast. Sometimes the monster is a personification of the sea itself, and it could also be used metaphorically to refer to heathen nations which threatened to destroy God's people (e.g. Daniel 7:3). Finally, it came to be a powerful symbol for the chaos, darkness and destructiveness of evil.

The most familiar example is the sea monster which swallowed up Jonah. Called a whale by the makers of the Authorized Version, that beast certainly represented death and hell by Christ's time – as when a Gospel reports him as saying: 'As Jonah was three days and three nights in the belly of the whale, so will the Son of Man be three days and three nights in the heart of the earth' (Matthew 12:40).

Jonah's fine prayer for deliverance (2:2–9) can be paralleled in the Psalms (e.g. Psalm 130). Like Jonah, we too will do well to make our own act of faith that God will deliver mankind from the monstrous forces of evil that threaten to destroy us: 'He shall send down from on high to fetch me, and shall take me out of many waters and deliver me from my strongest enemy' (Psalm 18:16–17).

Life Out of the Deep

THE Bible begins with a picture of the Spirit of God moving over an empty chaos of dark water which is without form and void (Genesis 1:2). Out of those lifeless deeps emerges the earth (1:9), then plant life (1:11), then the first animals (1:20). The primeval ocean is that from which all life comes – including our own, as the salt in our blood, sweat and tears should remind us.

At first sight there's a deep contradiction here. As we saw last week, the sea became a symbol of monstrous evil and death for the biblical writers: how could they also maintain that it was the very thing out of which all life emerged? The apparent contradiction was overcome by their fundamental conviction that God is almighty, and that, while going down into the depths means death by drowning for all that live on the earth, God 'ruleth the sea' and 'sitteth above the water-flood' (Psalm 29:4, 9) and is able to bring a new creation out of the deep, life out of death.

Stated first in Genesis 1, this theme reappears in the story of the Flood and its consequences, in the bringing of Israel out of Egypt by way of the Sea (Psalm 106:9–11), in the Book of Jonah, in the prophet's vision of the restoration of Israel from exile (Isaiah 51:10–11). It also appears in the New Testament and is fundamental to the understanding of baptism.

But it is important to remember that, for the biblical writers, this emergence of order out of chaos and life out of the deep is no natural evolutionary process, something which the deep achieves by itself. It is the doing of God through the agency of the Holy Spirit which moves on the face of the waters – 'a mighty wind that swept over the surface of the waters', stirring them up.

Such a stirring up is what we should pray for (if we have the courage): that God may again bring new life out of our chaotic world that is 'all at sea' – and out of the dead depths of our own souls.

Down to the Sea in Ships

THEY that go down to the sea in ships and occupy their business in great waters (Psalm 107:23) decide to launch out into the deep for a wide variety of reasons: some to enjoy a sail or cruise; others to fish, fight, ferry passengers and freight, or to flee enemies and find a new home; others to help those in distress at sea or beyond it; others again to explore and find out what lies the other side.

But the first ship mentioned in Scripture was the Ark, and the first voyage was undertaken not at the wish of man but of God. The Ark (the Hebrew word for box or chest) was a container ship designed to go upon the face of the waters and carry in its hold representatives of all living creatures to save them from death and give the world new life when that first earth had passed away and there was no more flood. The prototype ship was a unique lifeboat built and ordered to sea on the command of God.

The second vessel was also a lifeboat, though of tiny dimensions – a basket-work Ark of bulrushes in which the infant Moses was launched to save him from the death ordered by Pharaoh (Exodus 2:3).

Every New Testament mention of the Ark refers to its saving purpose (Matthew 24:37–39; Luke 17:26–27; Hebrews 1:7; 1 Peter 3:20), and it is easy to understand how the Church came to be described as the Ark – and why, to this day, the body of a church is called the nave (and *vaisseau* in French), and why the Early Fathers could maintain that there was no salvation outside the Church.

Most of us are not so sure about that. But there is still imaginative power in thinking of the Church as a ship, and of our life as a voyage; and we can pray for each other and all our fellow voyagers that 'being received into the ark of Christ's Church, and being steadfast in faith, joyful through hope, and rooted in charity, we may so pass the waves of this troublesome world, that finally we may come to the land of everlasting life' (*Book of Common Prayer*).

Catching Men

WHEN Jesus told some fishermen to follow him 'and I will make you fishers of men' (Matthew 4:19; Mark 1:17) – 'henceforth you will be catching men' (Luke 5:10) – he was making a bold use of those words. We assume he used them because they were words fishermen would understand. But we may be allowed to wonder what they made of them. Certainly they knew all about catching fish and why they did it: to get food. But how catch men – and why?

With centuries of Church history behind us we have become accustomed to assuming that Jesus was speaking of the Church's mission. And so he was. But it's not quite as simple as that. We don't find it easy to think in terms of 'catching' our fellow human beings by sweeping them up in a net – still less by enticing them with bait to come and get hooked. Is that what Jesus meant Peter and his companions to understand? If not, what?

In Luke's account the saying comes immediately after, at Jesus' bidding, the disciples (not without protest at the uselessness of it) had launched out into the deep and put out their nets – and enclosed so great a multitude of fish that the nets began to break. A similarly heavy catch was recorded by John on another occasion (John 21:4–11).

What did these happenings signify? Recall that earlier we saw that in the minds of the biblical writers the deep came to stand both for the realm of death and for the very thing out of which God creates life. In the stories of the stilling of the storm Jesus is proclaimed as the master of the sea in its destructive aspect; in the stories of the great catches he is proclaimed as he who brings life out of the dark primordial chaos of the deep – as God had done in the beginning. What Paul called the new creation has started, and Christians must further it.

Be fishers of men, Jesus says: catch people up out of the darkness of death and chaos and bring them to light – that they may have life, and have it abundantly (John 10:10).

No More Sea

TOWARDS the end of his description of his visions on the Aegean island of Patmos, St John the Divine tells how he saw a new heaven and a new earth, 'for the first heaven and the first earth were passed away, and there was no more sea' (Revelation 1:1).

Those who have followed these mediations on the significance of the sea will understand, I hope, what the sea meant to John and why it had no place in his vision of the final and eternal state of perfection. He inherited the biblical view of the sea as a powerful symbol for the chaos, darkness and destructiveness of evil – and there would be no more of that. He inherited, equally, the biblical notion of the deep as the primordial thing out of which God brought the whole creation – and, when the creation had been finally and perfectly achieved, there could be no more of that.

It should also be remembered that John was a prisoner of conscience, interned on Patmos because of his Christian faith. Life on a Greek island may be our idea of heaven, but for John it was more like hell; and the encircling sea meant what walls and barbed wire mean to any internee – isolation, loneliness and the loss of all freedom. And there was no place for any of that in his idea of heaven.

But we need not take John so literally as to suppose heaven lacks what the sea means for so many of us – the delights of the world's finest adventure playground. And the Lord will not take it amiss if, in a light-hearted holiday spirit, we give Kipling the last word. In 'The Last Chantey' he tells how God allowed the appeal of the jolly, jolly mariners against his decision to do away with the sea:

Sun, Wind, and Cloud shall fail not from the face of it,
Stinging, ringing spindrift, nor the fulmar flying free;
   And the ships shall go abroad
   To the Glory of the Lord
Who heard the silly sailor-folk and gave them back their sea!

Seeing Stars

YESTERDAY, in another world, I looked into another universe. It was no dream, no hallucination following an overdose of science fiction. These words are being written in southern Greece in September, and I slept last night under the open sky some five thousand feet up in the Taygetus mountains. All round were bare peaks and pine forest; no city's glare on the horizon; the nearest village six miles away and a thousand feet below; no human dwelling within three miles. The silence of that remote spot was immense. But more awe-inspiring than the solitude and silence was the sky overhead: a cloudless, moonless expanse of velvet darkness studded and dusted with the silver of myriads of stars – a spectacle now rare in southern England where the upthrown glare of city lights robs the darkness of its intensity and the stars of their brilliance. With such a ceiling above my head I was indeed in another world.

And I looked from it into another universe. Overhead was the constellation of Andromeda – and there was that faint, infinitely distant misty blur which is a spiral nebula. The book says that whereas all those myriads of other stars we see with the naked eye, the Milky Way included, belong to 'our' stellar system or universe, the Great Andromeda Nebula is a whole other universe nearly a million light years away and moving through space at two hundred miles a second. Telescopes have spotted over a million such 'island universes' all moving out and away from each other at speeds of up to 26,000 miles a second into God alone knows what emptiness ... I felt very close to the man who said to God: *I will consider thy heavens, even the work of thy fingers: the moon and the stars which thou hast ordained. What is man that thou art mindful of him?* (Psalm 8:3–4).

It is a healthy experience to spend a night, if only in imagination, in such remote silence and out of the man-made glare which conceals so much of the truth about ourselves, the great darkness in which we live and the magnitude of our own insignificance. As T. S. Eliot said, echoing another Psalm (46:10):

I said to my soul, be still, and let the darkness come upon you
Which shall be the darkness of God.

('East Coker')

FOR A CHURCH
DEDICATION FESTIVAL

What Mean These Stones?

A miracle had happened; the waters of Jordan had been wholly cut off while Israel crossed that river frontier between the desert and the promised land. A monument of some kind was called for. So Joshua had twelve great stones dragged from the river bed and set up in Gilgal; and he said to the people:

> When your children shall ask their fathers in time to come, saying, 'What mean these stones?', then you shall let your children know, saying ... 'The Lord your God dried up the waters of Jordan from before you, until you were passed over ... that all the peoples of the earth may know the hand of the Lord, that it is mighty; that they may fear the Lord your God for ever.' (Joshua 4:21–4)

What mean these stones? If only they could speak, they could answer the questions themselves. And what a tale they could tell, for stone lasts, literally, for ages. Paper burns, wood rots, steel rusts, flesh and blood decay – but rock remains. And so, whether stones have been used deliberately in the construction of monuments – as at Gilgal and in Trafalgar Square – or whether they have been used for more immediately practical purposes in the building of temples, palaces, roads and suchlike, they tell us much about those who lived on this earth in the past – about the sort of people they were, about the lives they lived, about the beliefs they held. As Jacquetta Hawkes put it in *A Land*: 'The centre of gravity of a people in any age may be expected to be found in the objects for which they will transport great quantities of building material.' Stonehenge, Roman roads, the medieval cathedral and castle, the

133

eighteenth-century country house, the nineteenth-century railway station or factory – all these tell their story about those who
built them. And it is a sobering thought that in the ages to come
men will learn much about us from the sort of works for which we
transport great quantities of building materials today: office blocks,
airports, motorways, atomic power stations.

Since you are keeping your festival today, it will not be inappro-
priate if we ask: What mean *these* stones which now wall us round
and which compacted together make up what we know as St
Margaret's or St Michael's, St Anne's or St Alban's? These stones
– for what do they stand? What can they tell us? What do they
mean? Let us exercise our imaginations and allow them to speak for
themselves. In general they say: 'We are what we are that you may
know the hand of the Lord, that it is mighty.'

If we press them to be more specific, they give us three answers
to our questions. Here is the first:

'We will begin' (say these stones) 'by asking *you* a question.
How old are you? Some of you have not been out of your nappies
for more than ten years, but most of you will not take offence, we
hope, if we guess that you are thirty or over. Most of *us* are
between 75 and 175 *million* years old. We belong to those ages
which you have labelled Cretaceous and Jurassic, when great
lagoons covered much of England, lagoons on whose shores lived
giant reptiles, dinosaurs and the like. For millions of years sedi-
ments slowly settled on the floors of these warm, shallow lagoons.
We – the clunch and the flint, the limestone and the marble which
together make up the fabric of this church – we are those sedi-
ments. It took some thirty million years to make us, and a further
100 or 150 million passed before we were dug from our beds and
brought here. Who was arranging, all those ages ago, that we
should now shelter you from the elements as you sing your hymns
and say your prayers? Him whom you call your God, by whom all
things were made.

' "What mean these stones?" you ask, and this is the first answer
we give you. We tell you this to remind you of God's greatness
and your smallness. Far too many of you humans today think too

little of God and too much of yourselves, and you haven't the wit to see that your colossal conceit is the cause of most of your ills. You need reminding of your insignificance. What visible remains will be left of you in 140 million years' time? Leave the millions out of it – what will be left of you in a mere 140 years? But for the grace of God, and at the most, nothing but a handful of bones and possibly a few teeth.'

So much for the first answer to our question. These stones proclaim the greatness of the Creator and, by contrast, the littleness of us, his human creatures; his eternity, and our transitoriness; his power and our weakness; his wisdom and foresight, and our blindness and folly and pride; his gracious goodness and our selfish wickedness. These stones cry out thus that we may know the hand of the Lord that it is mighty, that we may fear him for ever.

Now the second answer to our question, and again these stones shall speak for themselves:

'We have told you that that we are mostly clunch, flint, oolitic limestone, or Purbeck marble – but we now add that we are not shapeless blocks of these rocks; we have been carefully quarried and shaped and dressed; ton by ton, by land and river, we have been hauled here, some of us from considerable distances. And we have been brought all this way that we might be used for a building on this spot. These facts tell you something about those responsible for our being treated in this manner – those who built here over the last nine hundred years. They were *people of faith*. What was their faith? The particular kind of building for which they used us answers your question. They did not use us for roads or castles, for banks or factories; they built us into a Christian church. And they did that because they were people who believed not only that God is great and that humans are weak and sinful, but also, that God is love, and that men and women can be made strong and so become saints. In order that you humans might thus be delivered from sin and death and made children of God and heirs of eternal life, God himself was born into the world. He humbled himself and became obedient, even unto death, and then, having overcome the sharpness of death, he opened the

135

kingdom of heaven to all believers. He rose from the dead and ascended into heaven to prepare a place for you, that where he is, there you may be also.

'*This* was the belief of those who caused us stones to be where and what we now are. They did it that there might be here, in this corner of England, a house of God and a gate of heaven and an intimate home for all God's children. Here both the greatest and the least of you may have audience of the King of Kings in prayer, and may do him honour with your worship. Here, God receives you into his family at baptism, and here, he blesses your marriages. Here the word of God is read and preached; here you may receive God's forgiveness of your sins; here you may remember in prayer before God your brethren at their departing. Here, above all, is the altar which is both the throne of God and also the family table at which he presides and at which he continually gives himself to preserve your bodies and souls unto everlasting life.'

That is the second answer these stones give us when we ask what they mean. They stand here proclaiming to all who come in, and go out, and pass by: 'This is *God's house*. Do you really understand what that means? God bless you if you do. God have mercy on you if you do not.' They cry out thus that we may know the hand of the Lord that it is mighty and that we may fear him for ever.

What mean these stones? We come now to their third answer. Listen to them for the last time.

'Look closely at us as we now stand around you. We are very ancient rocks, we have been quarried and dressed, shaped and knapped, and we have been laid one upon another until we form one solid building, a house of God. At the bottom there are strong foundations, and the rest of us have been set one above the other; each of us rests upon those beneath, each of us helps to buttress his neighbour; each of us bears some of the burden of those above. Not one of us is idle, and all of us are held together by an invisible power and pressure. And we stand here like this to remind you Christians of what you should be. We are a visible model of the Church of Christ which is built up with living stones, each supported and strengthened by others, each bearing the weight and burden of others, and one and all held together by the power and pressure of God the Holy Spirit. We stand here to remind you of these things: that not only is God great and loving, that not only are you weak and sinful but yet capable of being made saints; we also remind you that God is the eternal architect and master mason, the only maker of unity, peace and concord, and that you Christians are living stones, his raw material "builded together for a habitation of God in the Spirit".

'First he gave himself to be the chief corner-stone. Then he quarried from the rock of human nature apostles and prophets for foundations, choosing first Peter, the rock – and upon them he built others. Ever since the work has gone on. Now, in this century, you are his material. And a mixed lot you are as we are, clunch, flint, marble, limestone. He has quarried you from the bedrock of human nature, and he is working away at each one of you with ruler and line, with hammer and chisel, with many a blow and biting sculpture. Some he finds easier to shape than others. Some are so tough, hard, resistant that you make his work slow and laborious, for you do not fit easily into the place in his Church which he has designed for you. Others of you do not weather well yet, but tend to crack and peel and flake away under the influence of wind and wet, frost and heat, soot and grime – the manifold changes and chances of this fleeting world. But his patience is endless and he will never give one of you up. He will always go on in the hope that each of you will finally fill to perfection your appointed place in his great Church; that you will rest firmly on those who have gone before you; that you will be a strong foundation for those who will follow you; and that you will buttress and support each other now, strengthening each other's weaknesses, bearing one another's burdens; and one and all so firmly held together by the power and pressure of God the Holy Spirit that no power on earth or in hell can ever divide you. And he wants you to be like this that those outside the Church, seeing you Christians and the love you have among yourselves, may know the hand of the Lord that it is mighty, and that they too may come to fear the Lord your God for ever.'

The stones have finished. It only remains to summarize what they have said. In both the baptism and the confirmation service, three questions are put, and the answers to those questions contain the heart of the Christian faith. This is the same as the answer to the question, 'What mean these stones?' Those replying declare their belief and trust in God the Father, who made the world; in his Son Jesus Christ, who redeemed mankind; and in the Holy Spirit, who gives life to the people of God. That is what this, and every church, stands for – it is the Christian creed in stone. In this, as in every church, the stones of which it is built bear witness to that beginning of all things at the Creation, and to the consummation of all things at the end of the world; and they bear witness to that unique life which gives point and purpose to all that lies between that beginning and that end – the life of him who for our sake and for our salvation came down from heaven, and was made man, and suffered and died and rose again and ascended in triumph into heaven, from whence he shall come to judge both the quick and the dead.

'Blessed is the King that cometh in the name of the Lord: peace in heaven, and glory in the highest.' And some of the Pharisees from the multitude said unto him, 'Master, rebuke thy disciples.' And he answered and said: 'I tell you that, if these shall hold their peace, the stones will cry out!' (Luke 19:38–40).

In their own way these stones here do cry out, that all the peoples of the earth may know the hand of the Lord that it is mighty, that they may fear the Lord your God for ever.

They that have ears to hear, let them hear what the stones are saying.

THE LAST THINGS

We All Fall Down

FOR all but the immature, the Fall is come in more senses than one. Leaves drop, apples drop, and all manner of other things are coming down as well – and the putting back of all the clocks in Europe would not halt, still less reverse, the falling and failing of this year, of the twentieth century, of Western civilization as we have known it, of old Uncle Tom Cobleigh and all. For all but the immature, sap time and salad days are over, brightness falls from the air, and the green and the rose are gone. Yellow and black and pale and hectic red are the in-colours as the wind whirls the leaves, and the cold and the dark come on, and the sound of the mower is heard no more in the land. It's lamps, not lawns, that need to be trimmed if we are to be ready for that which is coming.

We have been told not to be anxious for the morrow, for sufficient unto the day is the evil thereof; but he who told us that also spoke with condemnation of the silly young things who did not give a thought to their oil supplies and weren't ready for what was on the way. Season of mists and mellow fruitfulness this may be, but it's a short drop from ripeness to rot, and while there is still time before the fall ends and the crash comes there is an important work of collecting and conservation to be done, a gathering up of fragments that remain that nothing be lost, a filling of barns and larders and libraries and museums, so that all may be safely gathered in ere the winter storms begin, and the gates are shut, and the siege starts.

But there is more than that to be done. Indeed, that much by itself is appallingly dangerous if it tempts us to say, as the fool in the Gospel said: 'Soul, thou hast ample goods laid up. Take your ease, eat, drink and be merry.' There is more to be done – and it is *not* sentimentalizing over the past and regretting the fact that there is nothing in the world that does not fail and fall.

All of which may be a moody mixture of metaphors and no nice subject for a few minutes' musing. But, God help us, there is more in it than meets the eye. Atishoo, atishoo, we all fall down. So spare a moment now and again – and then again – to pray that ancient and basic formula: *Kyrie Eleison* – Lord, have mercy.

The Fall

Humble yourselves therefore under the mighty hand of God, that he may exalt you in due time. (1 Peter 5:6)

I will come back to Peter later. I begin with a lady. Her name was Eve, and there's a reason for that. But it might have been Alice – and there would be a reason for that. At least, alongside that story of the Fall in Genesis 3 listen to this extract from another well-known story – admittedly a good deal slighter but equally unforgettable, and not without value and significance when it comes to trying to understand what expulsion from the Garden of Eden meant:

She found herself falling down what seemed to be a very deep well.

Either the well was very deep, or she fell very slowly, for she had plenty of time as she went down to look about her, and to wonder what was going to happen next. First, she tried to look down ... but it was too dark to see anything; then she looked at the sides of the well, and noticed that they were filled with cupboards and bookshelves: here and there she saw maps and pictures hung upon pegs. She took down a jar from one of the shelves as she passed: it was labelled 'orange marmalade' but to her great disappointment it was empty: she did not like to drop the jar, for fear of killing somebody underneath ...

Down, down, down. Would the fall *never* come to an end? 'I wonder how many miles I've fallen by this time?' ... Down, down, down. There was nothing else to do, so Alice soon began talking again. 'Dinah'll miss me very much tonight, I should think!' (Dinah was the cat.) 'I hope they'll remember her saucer of milk at tea-time. Dinah, my dear! I wish you were down here with me! There are no mice in the air, I'm afraid, but you might catch a bat ... Do cats eat bats? ... Do bats eat cats?' ... when suddenly, thump! thump! down she came upon a heap of sticks and dry leaves, and the fall was over.

Alice was not a bit hurt, and she jumped up on to her feet in a moment: she looked up, but it was all dark overhead; before her was another long passage, and the White Rabbit was still in sight, hurrying down it. There was not a moment to be lost: away went Alice like the wind ... She was close behind it when she turned the corner, but the Rabbit was no longer to be seen: she found herself in a long, low hall ...

There were doors all round the hall, but they were all locked; and when Alice had been all the way down one side and up the other, trying every door, she walked sadly down the middle, wondering how she was ever to get out again.

Suddenly she came upon a little three-legged table, all made of solid glass: there was nothing on it but a tiny golden key ... but alas! either the locks were too large, or the key was too small, but at any rate it would not open any of them. However, on the second time round, she came upon a low curtain she had not noticed before, and behind it was a little door about fifteen inches high: she tried the little golden key in the lock, and to her great delight it fitted!

Alice opened the door and found that it led into a small passage ... she knelt down and looked along the passage into the loveliest garden you ever saw. How she longed to get out of that dark hall, and wander about among those beds of bright flowers and those cool fountains, but she could not even get her head through the doorway; 'and even if my head *would* go through,' thought poor Alice, 'it would be of very little use without my shoulders. Oh, how I wish I could shut up like a telescope! I think I could, if I only knew how to begin.'

Though without suffering much damage to herself Alice, like Humpty Dumpty, had a great *fall*. And it is usual for theologians to refer to what happened to Adam and Eve in the Garden of Eden as the Fall. In fact, though the word 'fall' is common in the Bible, it does *not* appear in Genesis 3 and nowhere in the Bible is it used of the happenings recorded in Genesis 3. The nearest to it is in Romans where Paul speaks of Adam's 'transgression' – literally in the Greek a sideways slip, a false step, a lapse. But when theologians speak of the Fall they refer not so much to the false step but to its consequence, not to the slip but to the drop that followed. In Genesis 3 that consequence is described as expulsion and permanent exclusion from Paradise. From enjoying innocent and carefree happiness within God's garden, Adam and Eve found themselves suffering pain and hard labour outside. They tumbled to it that they had lost something priceless, that they were in a hole, that there was no way of getting out of it. *That* was the Fall.

The act of falling, and the consequences of falling, are generally disagreeable. Almost the only pleasant falls are falling asleep or falling in love. Falling is disagreeable because, unless we are miners or pot-holers, most of us don't choose to go down holes; unless we are parachutists, professional gymnasts or divers, we don't willingly fall. For the majority of us, to fall off a wall, out of a tree, down the stairs, down a mountain, is to be suddenly *out of control*; without any warning, without any time to prepare for it, we find ourselves at the mercy of other forces and no longer in command of our own existence or direction. We don't fall as far as Alice, so we don't have any chance to notice the maps and books and things on the shelves around us. In those sickening giddy split seconds we have no time to feel much, let alone analyse our sensations. But if we could analyse them I suspect they would prove to be sensations of anxiety – anxiety about what we are losing and leaving behind ('Dinah will miss me very much tonight'), and anxiety about what the future is going to be. And if we survive and are still alive and conscious when we get to the bottom, then there's the question: 'How am I going to get out of this? I can't get up again by myself.' Holes are easy to fall down, but notoriously difficult to get out of. Anyone can drive a car into a ditch; it needs a crane or tractor to get it out again. The whole business of the Fall has a nightmare quality about it, the kind of nightmare in which you find yourself in a dark passage full of doors, and they are all locked, and the one key you have won't fit. Through a clink there's a glimpse of un-attainable happiness and freedom – a garden with beds of flowers and cool fountains. But you can't reach it. Paradise is lost. You can't even get your head through the hole – but what would be the use if you could? What's the use of getting through with your head – with that bit of you that's full of rational thought and good intentions – if the rest of you is stuck outside?

The truth about the principle of evolution, that human beings are descended from something like monkeys, as a factual statement about the genetic development of life on this planet, nearly all of us accept. The researches of natural scientists admit of no other conclusion.

But some go much further and hold that the fact of evolution proves that we humans are steadily and inevitably progressing upwards towards a superior state. Setbacks we may have, but they cannot alter the general direction of our ascent from lowly beginnings to something higher. But our experience of what twentieth-century man – man 'come of age', so it's said – can do and does do to his own kind, and not only to them but also to life as a whole on this planet, makes most of us hesitate to accept so optimistic a dogma.

On the other hand there is the Old Testament teaching that human beings are fallen creatures, who have come down from a higher state they once enjoyed, and that nothing but a super-human initiative can lift them up out of the hole into which they have fallen.

Faced with those two opposed beliefs it is not altogether surprising that the majority find the former the more credible. Knowing what we now know about our own past, the ancient Hebrew story of the Fall is simply unbelievable, not to be taken seriously. It is not just that the doctrine of the inevitability of our upward progress is more comfortable. The Bible story of the Fall is simply incredible. What justification is there for believing that men and women were ever in a paradisal state which at some prehistoric moment they lost? Can intelligent people today allow their understanding of human nature to be determined by a piece of Hebrew writing purporting to describe a Fall of Man at some particular moment in the past?

If we argue like that we have not rightly understood Genesis 3. We should not think of that story as a picture of what happened at one particular time in the past, but as a picture of a *continuous* happening to every Adam and Eve, every man and woman. This may not be apparent when we are young, but the older we grow the more we realize that it is *we* who are falling — that we are failing, are not what we were before. We get further and further from the comparatively simple, innocent, carefree happiness we remember we once enjoyed. We experience a growing sense of shame as we become more and more aware of the nakedness of our souls, a growing sense of guilt as we become more aware of temptations we've fallen into, and of good things we've left undone and so lost. But it seems too late now to save ourselves, and we have a growing anxiety about what's going to be the end of it all — for ourselves, for mankind as a whole, and not least for our 'descendants'. It's a hole we're in, and there seems no way out — lots of doors, but such keys as we've got won't open them. We have vivid glimpses of what life might be, visions of the garden of Paradise — but there seems no way whatever of getting there. The door is much too small:

which is another way of saying,
WE ARE MUCH TOO BIG;
too big for our boots,
too big to go through the eye of a needle,
too big to go through the door into the Kingdom of Heaven.

'Oh how I wish I could shut up like a telescope! I think I could, if I only knew how to begin.'

The way to begin is to pay attention to St Peter:

Humble yourselves under the mighty hand of God, that he may exalt you in due time.

God's Fireworks
– All Saints' Day

IN days gone by the *Book of Common Prayer* contained a form of service headed 'Thanksgiving for the Nation's Deliverance from Gunpowder Treason and Plot'. But it is 140 years since Parliament decided it was no longer proper to do such a thing, and therefore struck the service out of the Prayer Book. In spite of which, for every one person who celebrates All Saints there must be scores who will celebrate Guy Fawkes. It's not altogether surprising. Not everyone enjoys going to church, especially on a weekday in November. But however wet the grass, damp the air or cold the wind, fireworks round a bonfire are almost irresistible – fireworks in particular.

They are fascinating in their variety as they are exhilarating in their effect. There are those which make their chief appeal to the ear – the squibs and crackers and thunderflashes, whose glory is in their bang and of which we may say that they are of good report. Then there are those that are lovely and appeal chiefly to the eye: Silver Fountains and Golden Rain, Catherine Wheels and Roman Candles, Mines of Serpents and Bouquets of Gerbs – there is magic in their very names, but the magic of their names is nothing to the magic of their showers and torrents of sparks and stars. Above all there are the rockets and shells, rushing up with a hissing trail of sparks and bursting into coloured constellations high above the darkened earth.

The variety is fascinating; the effect is exhilarating. Not invariably, of course. The modern firework owes its origin and development to the science and sin of war. The very light over the battlefield, the maroons that announce the beginning and end of the two minutes silence on Remembrance Sunday, the rockets fired from ships in distress and to call out lifeboats – these may cause the heart to beat faster, but with fear or sorrow rather than with joy. Nevertheless, it is chiefly with occasions of rejoicing that we connect fireworks – notable anniversaries, the victorious ending of wars, or coronations, jubilees and other high royal occasions.

Fascinating in their variety, exhilarating in their effect, there is only one disease to which fireworks are liable – but that is quite fatal: dampness. The wet squib will not crack, the wet Catherine Wheel will not go round, the wet rocket will stay with its stick in the mud.

Whatever may have been the case in the Far East, fireworks were unknown in the Middle East in biblical times. Perhaps the nearest approach to fireworks in the New Testament is Peter's reference to an approaching persecution in his First Epistle; he calls it 'a fiery trial'. A few months later the expected persecution broke out. The Emperor Nero, perhaps just because he had no fireworks, was rumoured to have set fire to the thatched roofs of Rome. Alarmed by the reaction of the citizens, he quickly put the responsibility upon the Christians; and we have it on the good authority of Tacitus that the Emperor caused a number of those Christians, while still alive, to be dipped in tar, tied to trees and poles, and then set on fire to illuminate his gardens. The Roman citizens, like Tacitus, had no love for Christians, but both they and he were sickened by such calculated cruelty which used the followers of Jesus as human fireworks. And yet, in a terrible way, it was true. Those martyrs were Roman Candles. And it is not entirely unreasonable to suppose that, had the writers of the New Testament known what fireworks were, they would have likened the saints to them. Back in the Book of Wisdom its author had spoken of the righteous who shall 'run to and fro like sparks among the stubble'. Paul writing to the Christians at Philippi spoke of them as living 'in the midst of a crooked and perverse generation among whom ye are seen as lights in the world'. And Jesus himself, having just used a very homely metaphor in describing his disciples as 'the salt of the earth' and 'lights of the world', went on: 'Let your light so shine before men that they may see your good works and glorify your Father which is in heaven.'

Who are these like stars appearing? Who are the saints? Not only those whom Nero martyred, not only St Catherine on her wheel, but all the saints are the fireworks of God, fascinating in their variety, exhilarating in their effect. How bright these glorious spirits shine! How various they are! There is the goodly fellowship of the prophets. The prophets were those who, to put it crudely, made a bang; those who, by what they said and did, made people jump and sit up and take notice – like Elijah, Isaiah and John the Baptist. And there is the glorious company of the apostles and there is the noble army of martyrs – apostles and martyrs, those saints whom we commemorate on certain particular days each year, like Peter and Paul and Stephen and John, God's finest fireworks, rising like rockets from the darkness of the world and appearing like stars, high in the heavens, to whom ordinary people look up in wonder.

And there is that great multitude whom we commemorate at this season, All the Saints, some known, many unknown, men and women, of all sorts and conditions, as various as Catherine Wheels and Roman Candles, but one and all people who lived Christian lives of colour, crackle and sparkle. That is what distinguished them from the best of their good, respectable and pious contemporaries – the colour, crackle and sparkle of their Christian living. They ran to and fro like sparks among stubble. In the midst of crooked and perverse generations they were seen as lights in the world.

And as the saints are fascinating in their variety, so are they exhilarating in their effect. Who can read the true lives of the saints of the past – or meet a saint today – and not feel his heart beat faster? One and all, the saints are people who are fired with the love of God, let themselves go and allow themselves to be utterly burnt up and consumed for the sake of the glory of God, lighting up the darkness of the world around them. And the darker the world, the blacker the night, the brighter those glorious spirits shine, their whole lives spent unceasingly in celebration of the greatest of all victories and the highest of all royal occasions – the resurrection and ascension of the Lord Jesus. And whatever else we may say of them, we must say this of the saints – there is nothing damp about them.

'Let your light so shine before men that they may see your good works and glorify your Father which is in heaven.' We are not allowed to pretend that those words are only meant for a small hand-picked group of Christians in each generation. They are intended for all Christians. All, in Paul's phrase, are called to be saints. 'Let *your* light so shine' – not mine, or theirs, but yours. You are called to be saints. Fascinating indeed is the variety of ways in which, in the complex society of the twentieth century, Christians can fulfil the vocation of saintliness. That does not, of course, mean that God expects us all to take religious vows or become missionaries. Dons and doctors, nuns and nurses, students and secretaries, mothers and miners, pressmen and politicians – all can be saints. Some indeed in every generation are called, like the apostles and martyrs, to soar high into the sky; others are called to fulfil a prophetic function, to be Christians, who, by what they do and say, cause people to jump and sit up and take notice; but most of us are called to live our Christian lives in less spectacular ways, and in a simpler manner to shine with loveliness and to run to and fro like sparks among the stubble.

So to live is to give joy and happiness, to cheer and exhilarate the world, to cause others to catch their breath and look up and in the darkest of nights to rejoice in the greatness and majesty of God. But so to live means that we who are called to let our light shine before men today must at all costs avoid getting damp. The damp Christian, like the damp firework, has neither crack nor spark. Like salt that has lost its savour, he is only good for the rubbish heap. Yet it is so very easy to become damp and ineffective, and instead of creating joy to kill it. Too often, today as in the past, Christians cause the world to blaspheme rather than to glorify God, and cause it to blaspheme by being more concerned to censor such gleams of earthy joy as the world may have instead of outshining those gleams with the multicoloured sparkle of that heavenly joy which by God's grace they have it in them to show forth.

The good firework is not damp. It is dry as tinder, it is touched with fire, it lets itself go, and allows itself to be totally burnt up in producing that which is lovely and of good report.

Even so let your light so shine before men that they may see your good works and glorify your Father which is in heaven.

The Language of Silence

'FOR everything there is a season ... a time to keep silence, and a time to speak' (Ecclesiastes 3:1, 7), but most prefer the latter. Quite apart from the fact that we've got so much to say and can't keep our mouths shut for long, we find silence uncomfortable and embarrassing. Some people cannot stand it. They have become so inured to a background of noise that they've largely lost the ability to listen, don't know what listening really means or the value of silence and how much there is to be heard in it. Indeed, so accustomed have they become to continuous noise that, if it stops and stillness falls, they feel imprisoned, even suffocated by the silence. It frightens them, means nothing to them – is precisely that, *nothing*, just a terrifying emptiness.

In a somewhat similar way there are people who are afraid of the dark and hate going out into it alone without a torch. The dark means nothing to them; they think there is nothing to be seen in it; it's just a frightening emptiness full of the threat of unknown and invisible danger. But as most of us know, particularly if we have had the experience of being out at night in deep country, it isn't at all like that. Once our eyes have become accustomed and adjusted to the darkness we can see a great deal – including things which, like stars and glow-worms, we could not see but for the dark.

It is much the same with silence. Once we have become adjusted to it we find it is not at all the empty thing we supposed. All manner of messages may be picked up in it, including – if we are on the right wavelength – messages from the God who, in the words of the old collect, 'puts into our minds good desires'.

The Two Minutes Silence on Remembrance Sunday is never long enough. There's so much to be done in it, so much and so many to be remembered – and so much to be heard in it. But we've hardly become adjusted to it before it's brought to an end. Why isn't it longer? Because we couldn't stand it? Why not?

Monuments to Life
– Remembrancetide

MIDWAY as we are between All Saints' Day and Remembrance Sunday I am going to ask you to think about a particular saintly church and a particular war memorial which share the top of a particular little hill in the Belfort Gap in eastern France – the gap which separates the Vosges and the Jura and links the great valleys of the Rhine and the Rhône. Throughout history it has been a highway for traders and pilgrims – and for armies. And in November 1944, the Allied armies of liberation began to push eastwards through it to reach the frontiers of Hitler's Germany forty miles away.

The advance was desperately resisted, desperately slow, desperately costly of human life – and fighting was particularly severe on the little three-hundred foot hill overlooking the industrial township of Ronchamp. It changed hands several times. That hill had been recognized as a holy place from time immemorial, and for the last seven hundred years the small shrine of Our Lady at the top had been a famous place of pilgrimage. But in the fighting of late 1944 that church was reduced to rubble, and it was of that rubble that, in the 1950s, the great French architect Le Corbusier created a burial mound, a tumulus in the shape of a low pyramid, to be a memorial to those who had died in the fighting on that hilltop. Today that hill is visited by many thousands of pilgrims every year. But they do not go only, or even chiefly, to stand in silence beside that monument to the past; they go also, and chiefly, to visit another and greater monument on that hilltop – *a monument to the future* which in all ways overshadows, and is intended to overshadow, the burial mound, the monument to the past.

That second monument, also by Le Corbusier, has such power that it can be truly described as 'terrific', absolutely awesome. It draws people to it; it says something powerful to them; and they are sent by it. It is terrific, though it is only a pilgrims' shrine, only a tiny church. And you wouldn't know it was a church if the word 'church' suggests to you a piece of conventional religious architec-

151

ture. It has neither dome nor spire, Romanesque arch nor Gothic flying buttress. Small in size – a mere eighty by forty feet, and with seating for only fifty and made entirely of rough concrete – it is still terrific. It draws people, says something powerful to them, and they are sent by it. The Encyclopaedia Britannica describes it as 'the most important church of the past several centuries, so profound is its impact, so creative its force'.

How describe the shape of that small structure of dazzling white concrete which you see above you as you climb the hill? You can say there are three towers and four walls and a roof – but you have to add at once that there's little symmetry in the placing of the towers; that none of the walls is straight; that each has a different curve; and that the roof rises in an accelerating steep sweep up to one corner. Some might be reminded of a giant prehistoric cromlech with a single capstone perched at an angle upon upright monoliths; others might think of an upturned boat resting on the prow of a larger boat. But no such correspondence is intended, no symbolism to be looked for. Rather should the visitor be content to be drawn and captivated by the rhythms of different curves – curves that echo the natural slopes of the neighbouring hills and the undulating ridges of mountain and forest which bound the horizon in every direction; curves that are akin to the dynamic curves of the wings of aeroplanes and the bows of ships; curves, above all, which are akin to those found in those instruments by which waves of sound and light are received and transmitted – the curves of mirror and lens and television screen, of radar equipment and satellite tracking apparatus and radio telescopes. This unique church, a monument on a battlefield, seems to look out over all Europe and into space, to open itself to the universe and to draw everything there is towards itself. And the nearer one gets the bigger the pull, the stronger the signals. It is Power that is being transmitted – not through a rhythm and pattern of words or music created by an inspired poet or composer, but through a rhythm and pattern of surface and curve created by the genius of an architect. As such, the signals transmitted can be picked up by all – irrespective of age or sex, of tongue or nation, of race or even of religion. To the Christian pilgrim they spell an answer to the psalmist's prayer: 'O send out thy light and thy truth that they may lead me, and bring me to thy holy hill and to thy dwelling' (Psalm 43:3).

And what does the pilgrim see – and seeing, find – when he reaches the hilltop and enters the dwelling? At first very little. After the brightness of the wide sky without, the light within is dim and muted. Apart from the glow of the votive candles all the light is natural, diffused and indirect. It comes down the shafts of the three towers and through the thick stained glass of the thirty to forty small windows of different shapes and sizes with which two of the thick walls are irregularly pierced. As the eye grows accustomed to this gentle and sincere light it begins to notice the curves of the roof, of the walls, of the sanctuary step; that the bare stone floor slopes *down* to the sanctuary; that the eight simple pews are all grouped on one side only and face the altar at an angle; that the altar itself is not in the middle but a little left of centre of the wall behind. Nothing in fact is symmetrical. Yet equally, if surprisingly, there is nothing disturbing in the fact. On the contrary, it is very largely by such means that the architect has created in so small an area an astonishing sense of space and of total tranquillity. The walls are all bare, rough-surfaced, off-white concrete. The only other objects to be seen are a cross standing to one side of the altar – and a little seventeenth-century figure of Our Lady standing quietly in a niche in the otherwise bare east wall; it is the only object that survived the devastating cataclysm of the battles in 1944.

When the architect handed over that chapel to the church authorities in 1955 Le Corbusier said that what had animated him and his fellow-builders had been a sense of the Holy. And he added: 'I have tried to create a place of silence, of prayer, of peace, of interior joy.' Any of you who has been there will know that it is indeed a place of those four priceless things – and it is so because it is animated, inspired, as its creators were, with a profound sense of the Holy. It stands on a small area of ground which was churned up by a most bitter battle into a morass of mud and bone and blood. That that awful battlefield has been reclaimed and become for hundreds of thousands a place of silence and prayer and peace and interior joy is due to the fact that, under God, those who built it were people of faith in the future. They were animated with a sense of the Holy and its power; they built a pyramid mound as a monument to death and then went on to build a greater monument to life, that life which grows up out of death and sacrifice when we have faith in resurrection. In this monument on a twentieth-century battlefield all can meet a most powerful Presence – whatever their age, nation, race, even religion. To the Christian pilgrim that powerful Presence is the answer to the pilgrim's prayer: 'O send out thy light and thy truth that they may lead me, and bring me to thy holy hill and to thy dwellings (Psalm 43:3). The prayer is answered, and the pilgrim hears a voice, as it were, saying, 'Be still and know that I am God.'

But then the voice adds: 'Whom shall I send?' This also the architecture of Le Corbusier's chapel at Ronchamp does. It sends its pilgrims. It sends them in the pop sense of the word, giving them an intense delight through its sheer and still beauty. But it sends them in a wider sense – as bearers of priceless things to others. Silence and prayer and peace and interior joy are not things to be kept in a handbag for one's own personal use and comfort. They need to be carried far beyond the hills of the Vosges and the Jura, into all Europe and beyond. The world is crying for these healing medicines. Whom shall I send with them? Where are the men and women who will not allow themselves to become petrified by wringing their hands over the loss of the past, but who will allow themselves to be sent out from this launching pad to carry silence, prayer and peace and interior joy to the ends of the earth? Who will carry far and wide the message of faith in resurrection, in life through and beyond death – that faith so powerfully transmitted over the countryside of eastern France by that unique war memorial on a twentieth-century battlefield?

Ronchamp is remote to you? Perhaps. But if you are a person of faith in life rather than in death, then you know you don't need to go to Ronchamp. You will know – if the truth has not become hidden from you by the fog of familiarity – that every church says all that the Chapel of Notre Dame at Ronchamp says. From them too is transmitted an answer to the prayer, 'O send out thy light and thy truth that they may lead me, and bring me to thy holy hill and to thy dwelling.'

A church stands day in and day out that those entering it may find silence, prayer, peace and interior joy, and a Presence which says: 'Be still and know that I am God'; a Presence that adds, 'Whom shall I send to carry this healing faith to others?' It should be our prayer that we may have the courage to answer: 'Here am I. Send me.'

The Blessed Differences
– St Cecilia (22nd November)

THE first and last words of the *Te Deum* define what we go to
church to do: to praise God and to pray that we may never be
confounded, that is, poured together and mixed, merged and
mashed into one formless lump. We are here to praise God by
offering our distinct and different individual selves in contribution
to that single pattern of perfection which is heaven, joining with
the angels and archangels and the Blessed Cecilia, and all the
company of heaven and the four living creatures that rest not day
and night saying 'Holy, Holy, Holy, Lord God Almighty' – as
heard and seen in glorious audio-vision by St John and described
in the fourth chapter of the Book of Revelation.

Do not be deceived nor depressed by the snide remarks of those
who say that, judging by St John's description of it, heaven must
be much of a muchness, chiefly characterized by a great deal of
unending sameness, the last word in standardized uniformity –
monotonous, monochrome, monolithic, interminably dull and
endlessly flat. That's not what St John said he experienced. On the
contrary. What he experienced was a most luxuriant richness of
high variety. All the colours of the rainbow were there, together
with lightnings and lamps of fire, and the twinklings and sparklings
of precious stones, golden crowns and crystal waters. There were
thunders and trumpets and voices and different hymns being sung
concurrently and concordantly by different groups of singers. The
four living creatures were alike in having six wings and being full
of eyes, but in other respects as different as lion and calf and man
and eagle. And those four-and-twenty elders: when medieval
sculptors carved them over the doorways of Romanesque
churches, they surely got it right when, as at Moissac, they carved
each one of those two dozen old men as a recognizably *different*
individual – different postures, different expressions, holding their
musical instruments in different ways, different down to such
details as the fashion in which their beards were trimmed and their
moustaches twisted.

It is one of the divine marks of music that, while a composition is a unity and must have form, it is essentially just that, a *composition*: a putting together to form a pattern, and make a shape, of a number of different sounds provided by different instruments and different voices. To misquote St Paul, all sounds are not the same sound; but there is one sound of violins, another sound of violas, another sound of cellos and another sound of double basses – to say nothing of organs, woodwind, flutes, brass, bells, drums and all the rest. There are also celestial voices, and voices terrestrial, but the glory of the celestial is one and the glory of the terrestrial is another. There is one glory of the bass, another glory of the tenor, another glory of the counter-tenor and another glory of the trebles, for one treble differeth from another treble in glory. Which is all very trite, but serves to underline that any musical work, and not just a symphony – like any other work of art and like heaven itself – is an articulating, a planning together and uniting in one, of many sounds and silences, and therefore a composition of many distinct and different parts. To the work, and in the composer's intention, the differences are quintessential. To the layman some of those differences – the difference, for example, between A sharp and B flat – will be as subtle as the distinctions drawn by theologians. No matter. The differences are there. They are real, elemental, essential. They are not to be slurred, ironed out nor levelled down to one dull sameness. They are not to be confounded – that is, poured together, and mixed, merged and mashed into one shapeless lump. They are to be fully and faithfully maintained in all their singular peculiarities.

It is our fate to live at a time when there seems to be a great contempt of what is élite, a dislike of distinction and impatience with differences; and man's world – unlike God's world and God's heaven – is becoming as flat as a pancake, a world of rootless uniformity, soulless symmetry, mindless sameness planned by computer-controlled creatures who have neither face, name nor sex. Some differences in human society there certainly are which are differences born of evil and should therefore be destroyed – but destroyed because they are evil, not because they are different.

It is, therefore, a time when Christians – that is, people who believe among other things not only in a heaven which is a pattern of perfected differences but also, and more fundamentally, in a God who has deep differences within himself, so that he is at once Father and Son and Holy Spirit, three persons who are not confounded in one God – it is a time when Christians should be standing alongside the artists of the world (and not least the musicians) whose work it is to articulate and NOT CONFOUND the blessed differences; as David Jones never tired of proclaiming, to guard and maintain and compose into one all that is peculiar and insular, the holy diversities, provincial peculiarities, local singularities and the things which make each one of us an élite, unique and distinct personality with gifts all our own. St Paul's Cathedral is not Westminster Cathedral, and neither St Paul's Cathedral nor Westminster Cathedral is Westminster Abbey, the Chapel Royal or the Mansion House. None of us would have it otherwise – neither would God our Creator, who is 'a rare one for locality' (David Jones) and whose creation, composition, is witness to the fact that every single thing *he* creates is made unique – as the students of snow crystals and human fingerprints will testify.

It is no small part of the happiness and value of this feast that, to the honour and glory of God, and in commemoration of the blessed Cecilia, many different musicians, clergy and lay people around the world come together in worship to be *composed* into one joyous unity – a unity which has all the variety and at least some of the unity of the City of God and of the hills which stand about Jerusalem, a unity which has nothing whatever in common with that monochrome uniformity of the plain and the cities of the plain which the Bible calls Sodom and Gomorrah, the sewers of which drain sluggishly across the monotonous dead level plain to empty themselves into what is inevitably the Dead Sea.

But that is not our country, not the country of any artist, not the country of any musician, not the country of any Christian. And here we are, in company with St John and the four beasts, the angels and archangels, Blessed Cecilia and all the company of heaven – here we are composed together, to offer ourselves in worship to the thrice-holy God. We offer ourselves. More particularly we offer our differences and distinctions. We offer our samenesses as well, of course; but it is with our differences, the things peculiar to each single one of us, talents, voices, warts and all, that God is most concerned: with our evil differences that they may be repented and done away with; with our holy and blessed differences that they may be caught up into, and play their part in, that perfect composition, pattern and unity, which is the one Holy Catholic Church, the Body of Christ and the heavenly City of the One God, Father, Son and Holy Spirit.

We praise Thee O God ...
Let us never be confounded.

Fare Well

'FINALLY, brethren, farewell' – St Paul concluding the second epistle to the Corinthians (13:11). Of course he did not pen that word 'farewell'. The Greek word in the New Testament is χαιρετε – literally in English, 'rejoice', 'have joy'. Had he, as a Roman citizen, been writing in Latin, it would have been *valete* – 'be strong, have strength'. But the Englishmen who made the Authorized Version chose to use that word 'farewell', journey well – 'Have a good trip', as Americans say. For 'farewell' implies 'moving', travelling, making a journey. At its root is the old German verb *fahren*, to travel, which survives in our words thorough*fare*, way*farer*, sea*farer*, and in the term for the journey money we pay – the air fare, bus fare, taxi fare or whatever.

Fare well then: travel well. It is what of your kindness you now wish us. It is also what we wish you. For make no mistake, you too must be moving. All of us, always, day after day, must journey – getting ever farther and farther from where we were this morning, and all that is past, and getting ever nearer and nearer to whatever lies ahead in the future.

Leaving the past is often painful, but we are allowed to take some of it with us – not so much to remind us of it, but rather to preserve what is truly valuable of the past for the benefit of those who will come after us in the future. But it requires a fine judgement to decide what we must carry with us, and what we must leave behind, if our luggage is not to be so heavy that we cannot move as we should towards the future.

And just as leaving the past is often painful, so approaching the future is often fearsome – if only because we know so little about it, and because what we think we know about it is often powerfully dismaying. In fact there is one thing only we can say with certainty about the future, and that is that one day there will be an end. For us Christians that one end is, with the help, the grace and the mercy of God, coming to the vision of God. As we often sing at the end of the Eucharist:

Preached at the author's Farewell Evensong as Dean of Winchester, Michaelmas Day 1986.

From strength unto strength we go forward on Sion's highway,
To appear before God in the city of infinite day.

Keep that end ever before you, and daily and deliberately move
towards it – however hard, misty, bleak, painful and fearsome are
the marches still lying between it and where you are now. And as
you go, keep wide open the eyes and ears of your spirits that you
may recognize the angels who will be around you and hear the
messages they bring to you, messages for which the proper
response is always: 'Be it unto me according to thy will.'

I have often confessed the difficulty I have in deciding between
the frequently conflicting claims made upon us by the past and the
future. We are all aware of those conflicting claims, a dean perhaps
as much as any with his responsibility for the maintenance of so
august and marvellous a fabric as Winchester Cathedral, and his
responsibility for seeing that it shall also be made a place where
whoever shall enter it will find and know the presence, the peace
and the power of God, a place of true refreshment to each and
every wayfarer whoever he or she may be. Which should have the
greater claim upon our time and energy and other resources: the
conservation of the past or our concern for the future? And I've
tended to favour the latter, recalling that Jesus said with unmistakable clarity, 'Leave the dead to bury their dead' and 'Remember
Lot's wife' who perished because she looked back too much.
    But then he also said: 'Take no anxious thought for the
morrow.' And this has finally led me to the conclusion, which I'm
ashamed to say I ought to have reached long ago: neither the past,
nor the future, really matter. What really matters is the present –
what we pray and think, and do and are *now*, today. As the
Psalmist put it: '*Today* if you will hear his voice, harden not your
hearts.' Or, as T. S. Eliot put it three thousand years later:

> When the train starts, and the passengers are settled
> To fruit, periodicals and business letters
> (And those who saw them off have left the platform)
> Their faces relax from grief into relief,

To the sleepy rhythm of a hundred hours.
Fare forward, travellers! not escaping from the past
Into different lives, or into any future;
You are not the same people who left that station
Or who will arrive at any terminus,
While the narrowing rails slide together behind you;
And on the deck of the drumming liner
Watching the furrow that widens behind you,
You shall not think 'the past is finished'
Or 'the future is before us'.
At nightfall, in the rigging and the aerial,
Is a voice descanting ...
'Fare forward, you who think that you are voyaging;
You are not those who saw the harbour
Receding, or those who will disembark.
Here between the hither and the farther shore
While time is withdrawn, consider the future
And the past with an equal mind.'

('The Dry Salvages')

Here, *now*, between the hither and the farther shore, while time is withdrawn, consider the future and the past with an equal mind. Yes, it is now, the present, that really matters, today's stage in our continuing moving on. So journey well, fare well, *today*.

What is meant by faring *well*? Many things, but two in particular may be mentioned. First: it means having the necessary strength for today's journey, the strength we haven't got, the strength that only God can give, the strength to endure all setbacks, overcome all obstacles, and not least the strength to recognize, and act upon, the fact that, as Eliot put it in the same *Quartet*, 'the way up is the way down, the way forward is the way back'. As many a great soldier has realized, it is often essential to retire in order to advance. As any of us who walk in mountains know perfectly well, reaching the peak which is our object often involves a descent from the point we have reached, a going down into a deep valley and up the other side: it's the only way to the peak from where we are. To have to go down or to go back may disappoint us, dismay

162

us, even possibly be hurtful to our pride, and it will require great strength to accept the necessity and face it. Which, I take it, is no little part of the reason why a Roman, when wishing someone 'fare well', said '*Vale*', have strength.

But secondly, the Greeks of Paul's world, when wishing 'Fare well', said χαιρετε, 'have joy'. What is that joy? It is, I believe, the joy of recognizing that our onward journey is not only to be thought of as a march, a climb or a voyage, but also as a dance. Forgive me for ending by saying what you've heard me say before, that our daily Christian journey is not to be thought of as a toilsome advance along a grim groove of moral duty but rather as taking our part in a dance, following a pattern of ordered and graceful steps, a disciplined obedience to certain vital rhythms, a self-forgetting abandoning of ourselves to a pattern of movement led by the Lord of the Dance, our Lord Jesus Christ. Our immediate partners in the dance will change – the pattern of the dance, the Providence of God and the leading of Jesus will require that we release some hands and take into ours the hands of new partners – and that's all part of the dance and its joy, leading finally at the end to that heaven which is perfect life and perfect love, music and dancing, rhythm and melody, grace and courtesy, stars and atoms and beasts and flowers and men and angels – and all with Christ and Christ with God.

So finally, brethren, be strong, be joyful, and in that strength and that joy journey well, fare well. Amen.